The *Woman's* GUIDE TO MONEY

Also by the author:

The Prosperity Factor for Women

The *Woman's* GUIDE TO MONEY

Kelley Keehn

INSOMNIAC PRESS

Library and Archives Canada Cataloguing in Publication

Keehn, Kelley, 1975-
        The woman's guide to money / Kelley Keehn.

Includes index.
ISBN 1-897178-08-5

        1. Women--Canada--Finance, Personal. I. Title.

HG179.K43 2006   332.024'0082'0971   C2005-907619-4

The publisher gratefully acknowledges the support of the Canada Council, the Ontario Arts Council and the Department of Canadian Heritage through the Book Publishing Industry Development Program.

Printed and bound in Canada

Insomniac Press
192 Spadina Avenue, Suite 403,
Toronto, Ontario, Canada, M5T 2C2
www.insomniacpress.com

To Kathleen and Wyatt

Let us endeavor so to live that when we come to die
even the undertaker will be sorry.

–Mark Twain

Contents

Preface

One of my great life teachers, Dr. Wayne Dyer, in his audio program entitled *Manifest Your Destiny* tells a beautiful and profound story about a woman named Porscha Nelson. At a seminar that Porscha had attended, she and the other participants were asked to write their autobiography. She was asked to write her life story but it could only be the length of a page and she was to write five short chapters only. Here is what she said:

Chapter One:
I walk down the street. There's a deep hole in the sidewalk. I fall in. I'm helpless. It's not my fault. It takes forever to find my way out.

Chapter Two:
I walk down the same street. There's a deep hole in the sidewalk. I pretend I don't see it. I fall in again. I can't believe I'm in the same place. But it isn't my fault. It still takes a long time to get out.

Chapter Three:
I walk down the same street. There's a deep hole in the sidewalk. I see it there. I *still* fall in. It's a habit. My eyes are open, I know where I am. It is my fault. I get out immediately.

Chapter Four:
I walk down the same street. There's a deep hole in the sidewalk. I walk around it.

Chapter Five:
I walk down another street.

That's the story of Porscha Nelson's life. That's likely the story of most of our lives even if we haven't quite made it to chapter five to realize that we need a change.

The Chinese definition of insanity is doing the same thing over and over and expecting a different result. *The Woman's Guide to Money* will ask you to not only take responsibility for your life as Porscha did in chapter three of her autobiography, but it will also ask you to entertain the possibility of a chapter four and five in your life.

Have you spent a good portion of your life wondering why you keep choosing the same but wrong path? Perhaps it's a negative relationship, disastrous money management, or a job that you despise. Why do you keep walking down the same path knowing the deep hole is inevitable?

The first step is awareness. The second step is responsibility. The third step is a new path, a new street.

As you read the chapters of this book, I ask you to venture down a different street. Will you join me?

Walk with me in love, peace, and prosperity.

–Kelley

Introduction

In my career of over a decade in the financial industry, I had the privilege of getting to know hundreds of individuals and working closely with them on matters of finance. I had discovered that people act and think strangely when it comes to their money. I've counselled clients with multi-million-dollar portfolios who have lived more frugally than if they were flat broke. I've counselled clients who seemed wealthy and financially free of worries, only to discover in our meetings that not only were they broke but they were hundreds of thousands of dollars in debt. My clients were struggling with money regardless of whether they had lots of it or needed more. They didn't know how to spend it without guilt, or how to stop spending and still feel like a success. So if just having money isn't the answer to solving all of your financial problems, what is? Since I knew my clients needed more, I started advising them on what I call "foundational" financial planning, and it has become the impetus for this book.

As the architect of my clients' financial dreams, I was hired to put the finishing touches on their financial house—the doors, the windows and the decorating. But no one was taking the opportunity to ensure that the structure was built on solid ground or that it had a foundation at all. And so I set out on a path of dedicating my education to understanding the factors and beliefs that make us think and feel about money. I also wanted to discover how to go about making the life-changing actions that will free us from guilt and worry and help us look at money as a tool for creating the life we have always wanted.

The goal of this book is to help you explore your habits and thoughts about money and to start you towards a new style of thinking that will let you manage your financial life with pleasure and excitement, instead of with anxiety and stress. We will identify the hidden cultural and societal conditioning that you've conformed to during your life-time, much of it most likely as a child. And we'll explore a number of fun and effortless exercises to help you banish your limited thinking and develop a prosperity conscious-ness forever!

I know that since you've made the decision to pick up this book, you're a woman in search of answers, and I applaud you! You're also likely an astute woman that is serious about her finances and knows that financial free-dom is within her control. But I'm curious to know if you've ever bought a lottery ticket. Be honest; I won't hold it against you. Have you ever just daydreamed about win-ning the lottery and how all of your financial problems would be over forever?

If you have been guilty of indulging in the purchase of a quick financial fix, I have bad news for you: Did you know that most lottery winners, in just a few short years, become worse off financially than they were before they won the lottery? One needn't search further than the Internet, which is peppered with horror stories of lottery winners whose financial situations were disastrous.

Evelyn Adams won the New Jersey lottery not just once but twice to the tune of $5.4 million dollars. Today, the money is gone and she lives in a trailer. Also, William "Bud" Post won $16.2 million dollars in the Pennsylvania lottery in 1988 but now lives on social security. The night-mare of Bud's "found" money even led to jail time for him as he was arrested for firing a gun over the head of a bill collector. To add insult to injury, after his winnings were gone, he was over $1 million in debt. And such stories are not limited to the United States; in the fall of 2005, a Manitoba man hung himself after blowing $10 million of lottery winnings.

As you can tell from the sad but true stories of lottery winners, more money doesn't necessarily solve money problems. And if money can't solve your money problem, what will? What about the many immigrants that came to this country not long ago with no education and barely a functioning level of the English language who have retired either comfortably or very wealthy despite their humble beginnings?

Blood Money

Couple the inability to handle a financial windfall with the death of a loved one and the probability of disaster increases significantly. The largest bulk of our population, the baby boomers, are aging and are set, as a group, to receive the largest transfer of wealth in Canadian history; statistically, you could be one of them. According to a 2000 report by Capgemini, between 2001 and 2010, the transfer of wealth from the boomers' parents to the boomers was estimated to be $450 billion to $650 billion. In September of 2005, TD Economics estimated that over $1 trillion will be transferred over the next ten years.

When a parent passes away, the loss can seem over-whelming. The inheritance that "Mom and Dad" scrimped and saved for a lifetime is immediately given to the child by way of cash, real estate, or other assets. The parents had a lifetime to accumulate their wealth (no matter how big or small the fortune) and with little to no effort or financial education or experience, a new generation will be faced with this sudden gift of wealth. The problem? Many children see this passing of assets as "blood money." This is not just because their parents had a difficult time earning the money and had to sacrifice much more than this new generation but because the gift comes at the price of death.

I have seen clients over the years unconsciously push away this pot of money with laser speed and efficiency, and only in a negative way. I've seen children inherit homes only to lose them in a year or two by simple negligence. They might have an outstanding tax bill that was too hard to deal with even if they cleaned the house out at all after their parent's death. I've also witnessed foolish investment decisions, gambling, and other addictions as a way of using the money to cope with a parent's death.

The solution? First, we need to understand that money doesn't care—it's simply a currency or a conduit to that which you desire to use it for. The money doesn't become personified and we'll be exploring practical solutions in the early chapters on how to handle your current wealth, or lack thereof, and the possibility of windfalls.

It's About 90% Mental

I'm not a big sports fan. I enjoy playing the odd game of golf and occasionally watch a hockey game each year. But I do love taking in a few hours each winter watching skating. There's something so peaceful and elegant about viewing the athletes' performances; I like to think of it as ballet on ice. A number of years ago, I remember watching the Winter Olympics, and very shortly before, many of the same athletes had been performing in the *Stars on Ice* television shows.

During the Olympics, these athletes are at the height of their professional careers. They are diligent, focused, strong-willed, and have practiced most of their moves hundreds if not thousands of times. They have the best resources available including sports psychologists, personal trainers, and many others. So why then do so many of these skating professionals fall? Many of these skaters were at the top of their game during the *Stars on Ice* performances. They made all of their difficult twists and turns and landed with grace and ease nearly every time. So what happened at the Olympics? These athletes are truly the best of the best yet time and time again, I watched them miss easy moves and fall when there had been no reason at all to do so.

So what's the secret of the athletes who did succeed? It's called inner alignment. Diligence, hard work, and a will for success are all important ingredients to succeeding as an athlete or in life.

Wealth building is no different; it's about 90% mental. So why do we "fall" with our money? Why does the accumulation of wealth elude us? And why do we often make catastrophic mistakes when we have amassed money? Is our fate like that of the lottery winner? If we aren't congruent with our inner and outer selves, will self-sabotage and failure result?

Women and men alike are susceptible to money woes— so why did I decide to write this book for women? Women think differently than men when it comes to money. And now, more than ever, women are looking after the household finances and are taking on the stress, guilt, and worry of making ends meet. This is true whether the income is solely theirs or includes the incomes of their partners as well. And, more than ever in history, women have a number of reasons to be concerned about their finances.

Whether you believe this earth has been around for thousands or millions of years, you'll agree that it's been around for some time. For most of that time, men have been the providers and handlers of money and finance. It's only been since the 1950s, '60s, and '70s that women have had a hand in earning and handling money. And really, it's only been the last thirty or so years that it's been socially acceptable for women to handle the family's finances. Throughout the entire history of most cultures, this was solely the role of the male.

Couple our historical role as women with the primal instincts of being the family caregivers and it's no wonder that women are desiring to take responsibility for their financial future now more than ever before.

Before we move forward as a gender, I think we need to pause and realize how very far we've come. As a thirty-year-old woman in our society, I can't imagine a time of inequality. I was recently interviewed by a local reporter and her boss wanted her to interview a number of women entrepreneurs on the struggles of being a woman in business. Her boss assumed that my account would support the story's angle. After all, I was at one time an eighteen-year-old woman in a male-dominated financial world so I must have a number of stories about how difficult it is to be a younger woman in an older man's environment.

As we chatted, I couldn't think of one incident where I truly felt that I was at a disadvantage as a woman. Were there struggles in my career? You bet. Was it difficult to be a young woman attending financial conferences with the room 95% dominated by men and most of them over fifty? You bet. But all of my struggles in life and business were and are *life* struggles—issues that any person, male or female, would have had in the same position. Nothing more, nothing less.

Is this the truth? Is this reality? Would an onlooker of my life have viewed things the same way? Would they have identified some injustice that could only be experienced by women? Perhaps. I think of that age-old riddle: if a tree falls in the forest and no one is there to hear it, does it make a sound? If an injustice is committed but a lack of acceptance or focus on that injustice is extended, did it actually occur?

I know that it can still be difficult to be a woman in the workplace but it's never been something that I've even considered. If an injustice has occurred, I chalked it up as that of life, not of gender. But I can, in this day and age, choose to live a life of equality only because of the brave women that have walked before me. Not so many years ago, these women were prosecuted, spat on—and worse— for the equality that I and many other women take for granted today. I would like to share a number of accomplishments of these courageous women because if we don't pause and understand how far we've come, how can we ensure that it will continue for generations to come? We must appreciate the accomplishments of the past to truly move forward.

Did you know?

• After a long struggle, Canadian women (except First Nations women) obtained in 1918 the right to vote in federal elections after some limited women's suffrage was granted the year earlier.[3]

- In 1909, the Criminal Code was amended to criminalize the abduction of women. Before this, the abduction of any woman over sixteen was legal, except if she was an heiress. The maximum penalty for stealing a cow was much higher than for kidnapping an heiress.[2]
- In 1921, Nellie McClung was elected to the Alberta legislature, where she campaigned for old age pensions, mother's allowances, legal protection for widows, better factory conditions, minimum wage, birth control, and more.[3]
- In 1925, the federal divorce law was changed to allow a woman to divorce her husband on the same grounds that a man could divorce his wife—simple adultery. Before this, she had to prove adultery in conjunction with other acts such as sodomy or bestiality.[2]
- In 1930, another change to federal divorce laws allowed a woman deserted by her husband to sue for divorce after two years of being abandoned from the town her husband lived in before separation. Before, a woman's legal residence was wherever her husband lived, even if she didn't know where he lived.[3]
- In 1955, restrictions on married women in the federal public service were removed. In the past, female public service employees were fired upon marriage.[3] This occurred only forty-five years after a 1910 report concluded, "Where the mother works, the baby dies."[1]
- In 1969, the distribution of information about birth control was decriminalized.[2]
- In 1973, Pauline Jewett was the first female president of a co-educational university—Simon Fraser in Burnaby, British Columbia—a hundred years after women weren't even allowed to enroll or graduate

from most universities. Jewett went on to become a Member of Parliament focusing on issues of peace, disarmament, and women's equality.[3]

• In 1974, the RCMP hired its first female member.[3] This was one hundred years after an 1874 magazine stated, "Woman's first and only place is in her home."[1]

• In 1986, Sharon Wood from Canmore, Alberta was the first Canadian woman to reach the summit of Mount Everest.[2] Only a century before, women were discouraged from any sport by doctors who claimed sportswomen's uteruses would shrivel and they would become mentally ill.[1]

Source: Marika Morris. "Millennium of Achievements." Newsletter of the Canadian Research Institute for the Advancement of Women. Winter 2000. Vol. 20, no. 1.
1. Alison Prentice, Paula Bourne, Gail Cuthbert Brandt, Ether Light, Wendy Mitchison, and Naomi Black. Canadian Women: A History. (Toronto: Harcourt Brace Jovanovich, 1988)
2. Moira Armour and Pat Stanton. Canadian Women in History: A Chronology. (Toronto: Green Dragon Press, 1990)
3. Status of Women Canada, Canadian Committee on Women's History and Department of the Secretary of State of Canada, "Towards Equality for Women; A Canadian Chronology," Women's History Month, October 1992.

As women, we are making great strides and are moving to the forefront of business, money management, and so much more.

Did you know?

• More women are working than ever before. In the U.S., 99 out of every 100 women will work at some point in their lives and, as such, the problems of juggling family and work and making ends meet are increasing.
　　　　　–U.S. Department of Labor, Women's Bureau

- In 1950, only one-third of the U.S. labour force was female; by 2003, it neared one-half (46%)
    –U.S. Department of Labor, Women's Bureau

- By 2010, women are projected to account for 48% of the total work force.
    –U.S. Department of Labor, Women's Bureau

- Most "nonstandard" workers (workers who do not hold regular, full-time jobs) are women.
–AFL-CIO Analysis of Current Population Survey Feb 1997

- Women are also holding multiple jobs. In 2003, there were 3.7 million female multiple job holders.
–U.S. Department of Labor, Bureau of Labor Statistics

- Forty-eight percent of working women provide half or more of their families' income.
    –Economic Policy Institute

- Over a lifetime of work, the average 25-year-old woman who works full-time, year round until she retires at age 65 will earn $523,000 less than the average working man.
    –Institute for Women's Policy Research

- Women have less in pensions and savings and thus rely more on social security than men.
    –National Women's Law Centre

Women are continually making advancements and having an impact on our economy in new and exciting ways.

- There are over 6 million women actively using the Internet in Canada.

- Forty-two percent of Internet users are women.
- Women-led firms provide jobs for 1.7 million Canadians—more than the top 100 Canadian businesses combined.
- Women-led firms constitute almost one-third of all firms in Canada and are increasing in number at twice the national average rate.
- It is generally thought that between one-quarter and one-third of the world's formal sector enterprises are owned and operated by women, and that the share is even greater in the informal sector.

Sources: Beyond Borders: *Canadian Businesswomen in International Trade; Services to Global Markets: A Profile of Women Who Export Services; Myths and Realities* (Bank of Montreal Institute for Small Business); Industry Canada, DoubleClick Canada; The U.S. Small Business Administration.

While I worked in the banking industry, it wasn't uncommon to see a sweet, little, old lady on the other side of my desk. This woman was usually in her seventies or eighties and her husband had just passed away. She would come into my office stunned and distraught over the finances. She didn't know if they were well off, if they were in debt, or sometimes, in extreme cases, how to even write a cheque or make a bank deposit.

In the new millennium, I think within a few decades, we may find the sweet, little, old man sitting in front of the banker, after the passing of his wife, with the same fate. Since my first book, *The Prosperity Factor for Women*, I've had countless women and men tell me that it's actually the woman (more and more) handling the household finances. And many of the men that I've conversed with on this issue have happily turned over the assignment of money management to women.

So why is this such a big issue and why are women, now more than ever, concerned about learning more about finance? Think back in time, and, if you'd like, just the last hundred years. It's really only been the last half century or so, and particularly the last twenty to thirty years, that it's been socially acceptable for women to handle finances. It might be the case that for hundreds if not thousands of years, women guided or had some say in how the family's monies were spent, but it wasn't socially acceptable. And think, that for as many thousands of years human beings have been on the planet, again, it's only the last half-century or so that societies determined that a woman's place didn't have to be in her home and could be in the workplace as well.

In addition to divorce rates hovering around the 50% mark, many women are adding extra roles as parental caregivers to those of primary caregivers to their children. As a result, the average woman has a lot on her shoulders these days. Not only will she work more hours than she did just a few short decades ago, she will also continue to be responsible for most of the household activities, along with the additional responsibility of looking after her household's finances. She is less likely to have a pension than a man in the same field and will, on average, have far less in savings and have earned less in her lifetime. Women, more than ever, need to be concerned about their finances and need to establish a positive relationship with money—particularly acquiring it, earning it, spending it, understanding it, and attracting more of it into their lives.

If you're still unsure whether to read further, I'll let you know what this book is *not* about. The material in this text is definitely not about getting rich or accumulating a specific amount of money, unless that's important to you. It's not about how and where to invest your money, assuming you have money to invest. It's not about the teachings of specific retirement or estate-planning vehicles. And it's most certainly not about sacrifice, power, or greed. It's about freedom, empowerment, and acquiring the ease and understanding that comes from true wealth, prosperity, and abundance. And it's about helping ourselves, and others, and having enough to give to others freely. Examine the following questions and I think you'll quickly find out which answers you'll need to find in the chapters ahead:

- How do you define wealth?
- How often do you worry about money?
- How often do you feel guilty about spending money?
- Do you have a clear action plan for attracting more wealth into your life?
- What fears are holding you back?
- Do you deserve to be wealthy?
- Do you know what's most important in your life?
- Do your financial goals align with your values?

The strategies outlined in this book have been time-tested and developed from the experiences of hundreds of clients, course and lecture participants, and those that shared their stories from *The Prosperity Factor for Women*. I have had the honour and pleasure of learning the financial stories of thousands of individuals and hope you enjoy the journey and prosper abundantly!

Your Prosperity Action Steps

At the end of each chapter, you will find a brief summary of what you're learned along with a number of action steps to be completed immediately for maximum effect while the concepts and notions are still fresh. Statistically, those that purchase a book rarely make it past chapter two. Please stay with me on your journey to prosperity, not just by reading on, but by retraining your subconscious in a positive new way.

As you read the subsequent chapters, you will likely find that you're one of two types of people: a "knower" or a "doer." Some readers just want to know more, and that's fine. I can't force you to try the exercises within these pages. I have had the benefit of you purchasing my book and would like you to have the benefit of a full, prosperous, and meaningful life. If you would prefer to read the entire book first and then come back to the end-of-chapter exercises, they'll be waiting for you when you're ready. You'll also see a wrap-up checklist at the very end of the book to remind you of all of the exercises you have completed.

Continue to write in this book as space allows and I would also encourage you to invest in a special journal for the action steps to follow. Any blank scribbler that you have lying around the house would suffice but you and your future self are worth the investment of a beautiful and dedicated journal that you'll enjoy referring to and adding to for many years.

Chapter One
The Internal Game

This time, like all times, is a very good one,
if we but know what to do with it.
–Ralph Waldo Emerson

Although I hold no degrees in psychology or psychiatry, I have spent much time researching many schools of thought such as behaviorism, developmental psychology, and neurolingustic programming. One can clearly identify the patterns intrinsic in most of the researchers of the past; we have an imprint period—a time in our life, as early children and adults, where the learned behaviors of others are impressed upon our psyche. We can spend years determining what we've learned from our parents and other peer groups or we can solve our money problems (and others) by elegantly moving forward.

In chapter three, we'll discuss how what we focus on expands. If I were to suggest that we take an introspective look into our past and dwell on the negative teachings of our parents, society, and other rapport leaders, we might over time discover the answers. The following questionnaire is limited and its goal is to bring to the surface some glaring and somewhat obvious patterns you might have adopted from your past. We don't want to remain in the past but an oblivious attitude won't help uncover how we act today either. Let's briefly examine where we've come from so we can quickly move forward.

You'll notice a number of spots throughout this book that allow for introspection and writing. Please feel free to write directly on these pages. Use this book as a workbook of sorts and I'm sure that when you pick it up a few years from now, you'll be pleasantly surprised with how very far you've come.

Self-Assessment Questionnaire #1
Where Did You Come From?

1. What were your earliest thoughts about money?

_____

_____

_____

2. What were your early positive memories and experiences with money?

_____

_____

_____

3. What was your first limiting or negative memory or experience with money?

_____

_____

_____

4. Did your parents have a sufficient amount of money?

_____

_____

_____

5. If your parents had money problems, what were they? (i.e. not enough money, spent all of their money, were not able to spend their money, etc.)

_____

_____

_____

6. What did you experience from your parents' money problems?

_____

_____

_____

7. What positive learning experiences did you gain from your parents regarding money and wealth?

_____

_____

_____

8. What did you learn *not to do* from your parents regarding money and wealth?

_____

_____

_____

9. During your childhood and adolescent years, did your friends and peer groups have sufficient amounts of money? How did this make you feel?

_____

_____

_____

10. During this period, what did you think of wealthy people?

_____

_____

_____

11. What did you *not* have growing up?

_____

_____

_____

12. What did your social groups teach you about money and wealth? (i.e. religious groups, social clubs, etc.)

_____

_____

_____

13. What core beliefs do you remember growing up regarding money and wealth? (i.e. money is easy to earn; you only get money and ahead at the expense of others, etc.)

_____

_____

_____

14. Did you have a piggy bank or a secret storage place for your money? What was it? What did it look like?

_____

_____

_____

15. What did you purchase when you would empty your piggy bank?

_____

_____

_____

16. Where did you get money from when you were a child? (i.e. allowance, birthday gifts, etc.)

_____

_____

_____

17. Did anyone ever take your money or did you ever lose money as a child? If yes, how did that make you feel?

_____

_____

_____

18. Did you ever take money from anyone as a child? If yes, how did that make you feel?

_____

_____

_____

Our past is important in understanding our future. Inside us all is a child, a teenager, a twenty-year-old, and so on. Just because we've aged, it doesn't mean that these experiences are gone and forgotten. They live somewhere beneath the surface of our conscious thought. By writing down and acknowledging where we've been, it's possible that the simple exercise of doing so might lead to an unimaginable epiphany. It could shed light on problems that you've been unable to solve, but let's not get lost or create a helpless story from them. The purpose of acknowledging where we came from is to realize how far we've come and, secondarily, to realize how far we have to go.

Introspection can aid our awareness as long as we're careful to channel it positively. If we get lost in blaming ourselves, our parents, or others, we've lost the internal game. We have so much to look forward to if only we would focus on our goals: success, wealth, and prosperity.

We know that winning the lottery isn't the answer and that some immigrants that had nothing succeeded with whatever proverbial cards life had dealt them. But is there one sure asset or liability that the successful and failed share in common, one trait of the advancing immigrant or one glaring failure of the lottery winner that anyone could mirror or avoid?

Your Million-Dollar Ticket

What if I could offer you—for no money down, no interest, and no payments, now and forever—a multi-million-dollar machine? Are you game? I'm offering you a multi-million-dollar machine and it's not going to cost you a penny—not ever. Do I hear a resounding "*yes*"? Do I hear a "What's the catch?" Truly, no catch. Still interested? Well, the amazing thing is, you already own it free and clear—it's you! The gold mine between your ears—the amazing lifetime multi-million-dollar machine—*you*!

You are the only million-dollar investment that's an absolutely sure thing and you're already all yours. Think about it. Assume that you will earn an average of $30,000 per year from the age of eighteen to sixty-five; now, you're unlikely to earn $30,000 at eighteen but you're likely to earn more than that by the age of sixty-five, so I'm using that figure as an average. If you were to earn that much, on average, it would amount to a working lifetime income of over $1.4 million.

Let's daydream for a moment. Just play along with me, okay? Let's pretend that I really have given you a multi-million-dollar car. Maybe it's a car that Arnold Schwarzenegger used in one of his hit movies and it's been estimated to be worth over a million dollars. However, this car is so rare and unique that an exact dollar amount can't be placed on it—the value is simply more than a million dollars. Now let's imagine that you have just won this machine and it's yours, free and clear. Would you be jumping up and down screaming and yelling and calling up every friend you've ever known?

If we pretend that this event has actually happened and you now own this famous automobile, what responsibilities would you gladly assume with respect to its upkeep and maintenance? Would you take it to the finest of automotive detailing centres or would you run it through a gas station's car wash in order to save time and money? Of course, the first option is the obvious answer! Would you focus on the expense involved in maintaining and insuring it, or would you welcome the cost of such upkeep because it's going to protect this rare and valuable gift? Remember, this priceless experience and increase to your overall net worth hasn't cost you one cent. Who would be insane enough to quibble about the small details of maintenance?

One last thing, how would you feel as you walked down the street after you have hung the certificate of authenticity of this vehicle on the wall? Would you feel slightly more confident, perhaps even have a bit of a swagger? After all, you have a multi-million-dollar machine in your garage, even if the garage is falling apart and the inside looked like a junk shop before you carefully disposed of the contents in order to make room for the new vehicle. In subsequent years, would you take gripes from salespeople and negotiators or would you have the attitude: "Hey, don't you know who I am? I'm the girl with the multi-million-dollar machine at home." You might even have a bumper sticker on your current car announcing that fact.

So, tell me why we take our existing gold mine—ourselves—and our multi-million-dollar earning ability so lightly? Do we consider it to be less valuable because it was given to us free and clear? Why do we question the cost to maintain, educate, and refine its worth when it's us and we were born with it?

On the basis of the assumption that one could earn over a million dollars in a lifetime—a goal that even the average worker could achieve—why wouldn't we treat such a person, who might be yourself, as an extremely valuable person who has contributed to society? Why wouldn't such a person demand the best table in a restaurant or confidently ask for a discount at a hotel, even on a once-in-a-decade trip? After all, this person is a millionaire.

So perhaps I've commanded your attention and you're with me thus far? Maybe you'd agree that *you* are your most valuable asset and you own this asset free and clear, and you see that you might have been complaining ungratefully about the maintenance and costs over the years. Perhaps you're thinking that money isn't everything. So what if you're worth millions in a lifetime, what about family, community involvement, the environment, and spiritual growth? Good questions.

Defining Wealth

Despite working for more than a decade in the financial industry, I'm still a newborn when compared to many others. I've given hundreds of talks and lectures on the typical investment industry topics: RRSPs, estate and retirement planning, and so on. I have found that topics such as these are important but they don't make a strong and lasting impact on the real issues that people face when it comes to money and wealth.

Before getting to those issues, I'll tell you about the two clients who really made me shift my thinking about money, prosperity, and abundance. Two clients: we'll call them Bob and Tim. But first it's important for me to give you some background on their lifestyles as well as their net worth.

Bob is in his mid-eighties. He never married, he never had any children, and he's worth millions of dollars; he's a deca-millionaire. He could actually have a net worth close to $100 million but at this point it's difficult to tell as some of his holdings are spread throughout the world. Bob's age should provide you with a clue to some important background details. He obviously felt the impact of the Depression; if you could see him now, you'd see that he still lives in a state of fear that one day, no matter how great today is, his wealth could all disappear.

Bob made his money very slowly over the course of his life. He sacrificed greatly to build up what he has today and never measured his successes along the way. Then—poof—thirty years of scrimping, saving, and investing wisely and he's a millionaire!

The problem is, since Bob grew up during the Depression, he's held on to the scarcity consciousness that he was born into. If you saw him on the street, you'd fish deep into your pocket for a few coins to help him out, no matter how broke you were. He truly goes beyond the millionaire-next-door description. He wears only used clothes—articles that are torn and tattered and don't even fit. On cold winter nights, he'll double up on sweaters and socks before turning up the furnace as a last resort.

So what's Bob's purpose here? He doesn't have children or a wife to provide for after his death, why not spend a little, as his brothers and friends have encouraged him to do, so that he can enjoy his life more?

Now let's switch gears a bit. We're going over to Tim,

the total antithesis of Bob. I couldn't have imagined a client more unlike Bob! Tim is in his early to mid-fifties, is a professional, and has been earning nearly a million dollars per year for a number of years now. Pretty impressive, right?

Unlike Bob, Tim loves luxury and has, not one, but two very expensive luxury cars, spends time pampering himself at the spa several times a week, and loves to eat out on most days. These meals include elaborate lunches and dinners. Basically, Tim loves to live large! Tim's net worth? Close to three-quarters of a million dollars—but in the hole. That's correct; he's been earning nearly a million dollars a year and has almost a million dollars of debt. Tim has made many poor investment decisions over the years and these, coupled with an ego that demands attention, have created seven hundred and fifty thousand dollars worth of debt, and his goal is to retire in a few years.

> The mass of men lead lives of quiet desperation.
> –Henry David Thoreau

An understanding of these individuals should help to identify their subconscious or conscious views about money and lead us to examine the tendencies of each in relation to our own lives. Growing up in the Depression, Bob lived in fear of losing his money and therefore, at the simplest level of explanation, held on tightly to all that he earned, even at the expense of compromising his health (not turning the heat high enough in the winter and eating food past its expiry date). He grew up in a time of great poverty and had witnessed the experience of many in his community who lost all that they owned during those very difficult times. You must also remember that wealth in those days was visible and tangible—you could put your hands on it. It might have been a farm with an abundant crop or a successful town store, but generally wealth was on display for all to see. Not so in our current economy and for those such as Tim. It is possible to walk about and seem wealthy while credit-card and zero-balance investment statements arrive quietly in the mail.

Tim also grew up in poverty, although not to the same degree as Bob. Tim went through many childhood and early adulthood issues that lowered his self-esteem and instilled in him a mindset of insecurity and unworthiness. He knew that he could compensate with bravado and a public display of extravagance. His spending habits and inability to save reinforced the need for approval in his life. When Tim finally "made it" in his profession and his income was in the upper percentile, he still held on to his old beliefs of unworthiness. How could he therefore hold on to his wealth without some solid introspection? It's no great mystery why he would feel, at a subconscious level, the need to indulge in conspicuous spending. Many other issues and thought patterns are at work with both Bob and Tim and we will discuss these in greater depth as we move through this program.

When I looked at the two ends of the spectrum of what, on the surface, society seems to define as wealth—namely, financial security and success—I was disenchanted to say the least. I knew there had to be some middle ground between polar opposites such as Tim and Bob. I knew that it was essential to determine what made them tick with respect to money because I certainly wouldn't consider either of them to be successful and I am sure you don't either.

To have millions in the bank but live like a pauper or to earn millions in a short amount of time and not hold on to a cent of it, and even create more debt, don't seem like very prosperous, abundant, or successful situations. For this reason, I stopped giving just RRSP, investment, and estate planning talks and lectures. I was putting the horse before the cart! In order for my clients to learn how to save, hold on to their savings, or spend when the time is right, I needed to educate myself (and them) about the subconscious factors that drive us when it comes to money.

I always liked to think that my clients hired me as their financial architect. I tried to determine what structure they'd like to build—a house, a two-storey commercial building, or a large office tower. I then designed the financial blueprint to determine the specifics of the structure they'd like to build according to their goals. Wouldn't it be ridiculous if, instead of starting with the foundation, I spent all of my energy as their architect ranting and raving about the doors and knobs that they should order in from Europe?

Of course, one must first focus on the depth of the foundation for this structure. If we're planning a large office tower, it would be ridiculous to build it on the foundation used for a house. Under these circumstances, the tower would be likely to come crashing to the ground. Sounds silly, I know, but so many of us, including the professionals of the investment industry, focus on the "doors and knobs," if you will. Talking about and planning for the foundation isn't sexy or fun or exciting, but it will support our structure in the long term. Most people don't even determine the type or size of the financial structure they'd like to build, so how can they possibly understand the foundation necessary for long-term strength and viability?

So, if you've determined from my earlier example that you don't want to be like either Bob or Tim, but that you, like most North Americans, would like to be wealthy, here's the magic question: How will you know if you're wealthy? What indications will you see in your life—luxury cars, a grand home, a large balance on your financial statement? When will you feel secure and free and hear the praises of your friends, family, and community? How will you know when you've arrived at your goal if the goal is vague and unclear?

Your personal foundation comprises all of the past references, beliefs, and experiences about money and prosperity that you hold to be true in your conscious and subconscious mind. This base will determine the type of structure you'll build, its strength, and its ability to remain strong.

The problem with (and the great thing about) the vagueness of such ideas as wealth, success, and abundance is that you have the opportunity to define these ideas as you choose. For you, being wealthy might mean having millions of dollars in the bank. Perhaps wealth means just having enough to be able to live comfortably and allow you to make a big difference on this planet through your works of philanthropy and volunteerism. It's up to you. It's as personal and individual as what type of meal you prefer to eat.

We will spend more time and detail in defining what success and wealth look like to you in chapter six but for now I'd like you to ponder the following poem. The poetic words written by Sir Edward Dyer (1543–1607) expand my definition of success and wealth as I hope they will yours. Pay particular attention to stanzas four, five, and six.

My Mind to Me a Kingdom Is

My mind to me a kingdom is;
Such perfect joy therein I find
That excels all other bliss
Which God or nature hath assign'd.
Though much I want that most would have,
Yet still my mind forbids to crave.

No princely port, nor wealthy store,
No force to win a victory,
No wily wit to salve a sore,
No shape to win a loving eye;
To none of these I yield as thrall, —
For why? my mind despise them all.

I see that plenty surfeit oft,
And hasty chambers soonest fall;
I see that such as are aloft
Mishap doth threaten most of all.

These get with toil and keep with fear;
Such cares my mind can never bear.

I press to bear no haughty sway,
I wish no more than may suffice,
I do no more than well I may,
Look, what I want my mind supplies.
Lo! thus I triumph like a king,
My mind content with anything.

I laugh not at another's loss,
Nor grudge not at another's gain;
No worldly waves my mind can toss;
I brook that is another's bane.
I fear no foe, nor fawn on friend,
I loathe not life, nor dread mine end.

My wealth is health and perfect ease,
And conscience clear my chief defense;
I never seek by bribes to please,
Nor by desert to give offence.
Thus do I live, thus will I die, —
Would all did so as well as I!

Self-Worth vs. Net Worth

Have you ever measured your self-worth according to your financial state? Are you waiting to feel better about yourself and your life when, one day, your net worth increases to a certain level? There's great danger in linking our worth to the size of the financial rewards we have or one day hope to have. Money may come and go in our lives but our worth is something that should be independent of the bottom line on our balance sheet.

I'm reminded of a local businessman in Edmonton whose abilities had garnered great international acclaim. His business acumen failed him over time and his empire was crumbling at his feet. Many people in our city either loved or hated this man but I felt sorry for him as the media hounded him at the hour of his despair. The television cameras were there while his personal belongings, including his wine collection, were being removed from his home. The camera zoomed in as the reporter asked him how he was coping with losing his fortune and with the humiliation of his imminent bankruptcy. The businessman, dressed in his finest suit and sipping on a glass of champagne, simply replied, "My self-worth isn't defined by my net worth."

I have personally known individuals who have amassed large amounts of financial wealth only to lose it all. Whether such people could get back on their feet again depended on whether their worth rested solely on their financial gains or on their sense of the sort of person they had become on the journey. Many great people of our time have lost it all and built back even greater fortunes but they could do so only as long as they hadn't defined their personal worth in financial terms. You need only look at Donald Trump. There was a time when he lost his fortune and the media took great pleasure in writing stories about the fall of the New York giant. But now "The Donald" is back and bigger than ever. Love him or hate him, he knows the secret of defining his worth as more than a dollar figure.

Watch Your Pennies Carefully Because the Dollars Might Kill You

Money (or the lack thereof) can kill a person. Common sense supports such a statement because someone could rob an individual of their money, break into their house, or commit many other acts of violence in the procurement of someone else's fortune. Mine is a tale of financial heartbreak that indirectly lead to the death of a close friend of mine. During the last decade of his life, I'm sure that he never realized that the lack of money had broken his heart. But hindsight is 20/20 as they say and should you have witnessed the life of this fellow, you would have come to the same conclusion as I. We'll call him Emerson.

Emerson was a wonderfully kind-hearted man who worked hard all of his life. For whatever reason, he just couldn't "handle" money. He always filed his taxes late, if at all, and many times in his life he was years behind and would only file at the urging of his wife. This procrastination later turned to fear and he also invested his money in a safety deposit box at his local bank, thereby letting inflation and the absence of any investment interest erode his savings over time. Emerson always insisted that his wife handle their money and turned a blind eye when she would go on her regular spending sprees. He never planned for the future and was afraid to face the present.

When Emerson's wife died, he entrusted the handling of his savings within the safety deposit box to his daughter. To escape the pain of the passing of his wife, he moved back to the city which he'd left over twenty years ago. Whenever he needed money, he'd take a short trip back to see his daughter, which would carry him financially until the next trip.

Finally, after a number of years, Emerson's grief for his wife started to wane. He met a new love, let her into his life, and his retirement had a promising future. Emerson travelled with his new love, dined out, and his life showed promise and renewed vigor. It was time for one of those trips to his daughter's again to fill up his coffers. He travelled with his love to take out a deposit, and to his chagrin, almost all of the money was gone. There was a meagre pittance of funds left, perhaps enough for him to live comfortably for only a year or two. Without questioning his daughter's money management or ethics, Emerson left heartbroken.

Back home, he dusted himself off and got a part-time job. But only weeks later, Emerson's tired body started to ache and he knew that at his ripe age, he was no longer able to work. Luckily for Emerson, his new love had some resources and a home which he could move into rent-free to reduce the burden on him financially. Within a year, Emerson had a major stroke that rendered him feeble and banished him to bedrest with his love providing the caregiving.

Two hard years passed and Emerson faced numerous smaller strokes until he was unable to speak, walk, or take care of himself at all. Months later, Emerson passed away without even enough to pay for his funeral.

Did the lack of money break Emerson's heart and lead to his death? Certainly no autopsy would prove such findings. But as we explore self-worth and its relationship to net worth, I can assure you that Emerson defined his manhood and worth on this planet primarily in terms of to his ability to at least provide for himself and his family. He could have also taken control of his finances and not let the numbers intimidate him, but he chose otherwise.

Emerson's story teaches us that we need to take responsibility for our financial security. Failure to do so will not likely kill you but it certainly might affect your overall self-esteem and self-worth regarding wealth.

The History of Money

Just as the introduction of this book looked at the history of women and the challenges we've faced as a gender, we must also look at the history of money. A better understanding of the origins of money can help us make the decision of what we'd like it to mean for us today and in the future.

> Riches may enable us to confer favours,
> but to confer them with propriety and grace
> requires a something that riches cannot give.
> –Charles Caleb Colton

The term *money* conjures up many thoughts, beliefs, and images, both positive and negative. Money is scarce by its very nature. Even if you subscribe to a prosperity consciousness, one must admit to money's inadequacy as there's not enough of it to fulfill everyone's wants and needs. When a resource is scare, it's more sought after and valuable. I find it ironic, however, that in Greek, *money* is loosely translated to mean something we think has value, or something that someone convinced us has, but in reality it doesn't.

Money used to comprise such items as gold, silver, and other precious metals; salt, pepper, and other spices; and even tobacco. In medieval Iraq, bread was used as an early form of currency. Today, money primarily takes the form of a bank note. A bank note is called a bill in the U.S. and Canada and is used as legal tender. Originally, money was backed by silver or gold but carrying around large amounts of precious metals didn't make sense and could also be dangerous. As an alternative, bank notes came about.

A note is a promise to pay someone money. Notes were originally a promise to pay the bearer an amount of precious metals stored in a vault somewhere. This is no longer true today. Our currency is now fiat money and not backed by gold or silver. As bank notes became more widely used, they became more accepted as equivalent to precious metals. Bank notes are now simply called money.

Bad Money Drives Out Good Money

We've all heard the saying "throw good money after bad," as if money could be good or bad. Money "just is," no matter how much we try to personify it. We'll look more at the personification of money in chapter two.

The phrase "bad money drives out good money" comes from an ancient time when coins were fashioned by shaving—where precious metals were removed from the coins, leaving them useful as an identifiable unit in the marketplace. It was first observed by Copernicus, and later in 1558 by Sir Thomas Gresham. Gresham's law states that "where legal tender law exists, bad money draws out good money."

A common explanation of Gresham's law is that people will always keep the coin that is in better condition (less clipped, less filed) and offer the less attractive one in the marketplace first even though the same value exists. It is only a matter of time before the "bad" coins become extinct and the good ones are retained. (Source: Wikipedia.)

Have you ever received an unusually tattered bill of money; the type that looks like it went to the courtyard after school for a brawl and lost; the type that's barely hanging on with Scotch tape on both sides? I'm not sure about your experience, but that's the bill that I always try to get rid of first. Somehow, a ragged twenty dollar bill, perhaps graffitied with writing of some type, seems to have less worth than a crisp fresh one from the bank teller or ATM.

The History of Credit Cards

In the new millennium, it seems as important to examine the history of credit cards as the history of money. As a member of the Generation X demographic, I'm saddened to admit that paying with plastic (whether debit or credit card) has superseded paying with real money. A history is indeed in order!

> I'm living so far beyond my income that
> we may almost be said to be living apart.
> –e. e. cummings

The first credit card was actually created in the 1920s and was used to sell fuel to a growing number of car owners. Frank X. McNamara came up with the concept of paying merchants using a card in 1950. The first charge card in existence was the Diners Club.

In 1958, Bank of America introduced their card which evolved into the Visa system, and MasterCard followed suit in 1966. There is now a countless number of cards in the U.S. and Canada that are almost universally accepted in both countries. An economic agreement can be made whereby using credit cards increases the velocity of money in an economy, resulting in higher consumer spending, escalating debt, and higher GDP. Credit-card debt has soared to new heights in the last decade and I'm sure we all know someone that has had to bear the tragedy of being unable to handle such debts. (Source: Wikipedia.)

I sat down with a friend and client some time ago over a three-hour Greek dinner. My friend has lived in Canada for about ten years but grew up and lived in a number of European cities and needed my advice about how to get out of the financial debt he had incurred in just a few short years. He shared with me a past life that a Canadian-born girl could only dream of. He described the normal work-day routine in his hometown as the following: everyone comes down out of their apartments in the morning around 8 or 9 a.m. and there are tables, coffee merchants, and vendors on every street. Most citizens sip their coffee and chat with friends and strangers until mid-morning. Then it's time for work but the day breaks in the mid to late afternoon. Then, they go back to work for a couple of hours and break again for dinner and likely a little entertainment or partying for the evening.

I'm sure that my friend's experience and memories of Europe are not the same as all who live or have lived there, but I did find his account of his life in Canada just a decade later quite interesting. My friend told me that in the European cities he lived in, few of his friends, family members, or associates from work had a car or a home that they owned. He revealed to me that the average person didn't have aspirations of ever owning a home or if they did, it wouldn't be large or elaborate. The accepted norm within his peer group was also to walk or take public transit, so a car and all of the costs associated with owning one wasn't a goal of his in Europe.

Fast forward to approximately ten years ago after he arrived in Canada and found a new set of friends, peer groups, and work associates. He was a little shocked at how hard everyone worked to pay for their "things" and at the end of the day, instead of long elaborate dinners and nights of dancing, his friends barely made it home to plop in front of their TVs before drifting off to bed.

He allowed himself to immerse fully in his Canadian

environment and within a year, had bought himself a home that he could barely afford. Within a couple more years, he married, had two cars, one child, and a family with one income.

Over souvlaki and many other Greek delights, he vented to me how he was now the "average" Canadian. He still couldn't figure out why our society was more concerned with what we *have* in life as opposed to our *quality* of life, but he admitted that, like his peers in Europe, he followed the crowd. And like so many North Americans, he traded in his morning coffee and evenings of enjoyment for the things he felt were more important.

Definitions for Life

Throughout the pages of this book, we will further explore the meanings of *money* and *riches* but we will focus mostly on *wealth*, *abundance*, and *prosperity*, all of which encompass so much more than just monetary gain. I think it's important to start with the very basics and ensure that we understand the literal meanings of these words, then you can redefine them to fit your own life. Below are a number of important words that I encourage you to define. Should you not have a dictionary close at hand, two of the greatest resources on the Internet today are www.dictionary.com and www.wikipedia.org. Please use several sources for defining the following words and aim to understand what these words mean in general and what they specifically mean to you.

Money:

_____

_____

_____

Currency:

_____

_____

_____

Rich:

_____

_____

_____

Wealth:

_____

_____

_____

Prosperity:

_____

_____

_____

Abundance:

_____

_____

_____

> All life is an experiment.
> –Ralph Waldo Emerson

Summary

- You have the ability to earn over a million dollars in your lifetime and you are the most important investment that you will ever make. Live and act like a millionaire.
- Determine what type of financial building is right for you. The larger the structure, the more time you'll need to invest in creating a strong foundation.
- Don't make the mistakes that Bob and Tim made. Keep reading the remainder of this book to learn how to save and spend your money comfortably and intelligently.
- Support yourself in being wealthy by choosing your words carefully, especially those that surround your ability to prosper.

- Remember that self-worth and net worth are independent notions.

Your Prosperity Action Steps

This chapter is an easy one; I only have two action steps for you and I hope that you've already completed the first one.

- Please make sure you've taken time to complete the Self-Assessment Questionnaire.
- Find a blank scribbler and preferably a lovely blank journal for the action steps in the following chapters.

Chapter Two
Let's Play

Nothing splendid has ever been achieved except
by those who dared believe that something
inside of them was superior to circumstance.
–Bruce Barton

In chapter one, I asked that you look back at your childhood and your parents and peer groups to identify clues as
to where your thoughts and beliefs about money came
from. In this next chapter, I would like you to look at where
you are now. This might seem a difficult task at the onset
but I assure you that the clarity of understanding of where
you are today will propel you to where you'd like to go.
Think of this exercise as a simple calculation; you likely
have not achieved all of your financial goals or at the very
least are interested in improving your wealth. To get from
point A—where you are today—to point B—where you'd
like to be in the future—we need to first identify point A.
Sounds simple enough but it's the "doing" that is the first
step on any path to success. Furthermore, when you have
reached point B, you'll have a record of how very far
you've come. I encourage you to complete the following
short questionnaire on an annual basis. Then, as I will
guide you in chapter five, I would also encourage you to
re-evaluate your point B. You might discover that in a short
period of time you'll need to create higher goals for which
to reach.

Self-Assessment Questionnaire #2
Where Are You Now?

1. What are your current core thoughts and beliefs about money?

_____

_____

_____

2. Do these thoughts and beliefs differ from your answers in the first self-assessment questionnaire? If so, how?

_____

_____

_____

3. Where are these thoughts and beliefs coming from? (i.e. old thoughts, peer groups, spouse, others.)

_____

_____

_____

4. What is your current net worth (your assets minus your liabilities/debts)?

_____

5. What is your current annual income?

_____

6. When was the last time you experienced pleasure from money? Describe the situation.

_____

_____

_____

7. When was the last time you bought something for yourself? What was it and how did it make you feel?

_____

_____

_____

Do You Have A Problem with Money?

The question: Are you willing to be wealthy? Take a moment now to ask yourself that question out loud. Or better yet, take out pen and paper and write it down. As Frederic Lehrman encourages his listeners to ask in his wonderful audio program *Prosperity Consciousness*, *"Am I willing to be wealthy?"* What do you hear back? A resounding "yes," a resounding "no," maybe something in between? I remember the first time I tried this exercise. The first time I recited the sentence back to myself, a loud voice in my head exclaimed, "Yes! Darn right, I deserve to be wealthy!" And then I went about my day, weeks, and life without much conscious thought as to what I had stirred up deep within me.

Then, several weeks later, and quite literally out of nowhere, some old and long-forgotten thoughts started creeping into my consciousness—thoughts like: But if you're wealthy, you'll be evil; if you're wealthy, you won't love God as much and he might not love you. Many of us have heard time and again that "money is the root of all evil" when the actual Biblical quote is "the love of money is the root of all evil" (Timothy 6:10).

The great thing about this was that these thoughts were now in my consciousness so I could examine them, their origins, and my choice to believe them still. I remembered the many misinformed and irrational teachings of my church, my childhood teachers, and my family; all those disseminated beliefs that were still lurking in my subconscious. And since so many of these notions were taught to me as a young child, I likely had skewed, deleted, or added to those early teachings. I had much research to do as an adult, and not as that five-year-old who attended Sunday school and who still lives within me.

> Judge a man by his questions
> rather than his answers.
> –Voltaire

Ask yourself if you're willing to be wealthy many times throughout a period of several weeks, and whether your first answer was an immediate "yes" or an immediate "no," see if that answer changes over time. Does that voice within you say something different in the weeks ahead? How do you feel as you ask this question of yourself?

You could just as easily ask yourself the question, "Do I deserve to be healthy?" or "Do I deserve to be happy?" If you haven't taken a few seconds to write these questions down, please do. And then take your finger and simply cover the last word—the word "wealthy," or "healthy," or "happy." Now you're left with, "Do I deserve to *be*?" Now take this question seriously because if you don't feel worthy of your own existence, how could you ever feel worthy of wealth, happiness, or perfect health? We will spend the last few chapters dealing with self-worth and self-esteem in greater detail. It might seem like an unusual inclusion for a book about money and prosperity but if we don't love and appreciate ourselves, how could we ever attract more money into our lives or be happy when more money does show up?

> The worst loneliness is not to be
> comfortable with yourself.
> –Mark Twain

This will be one of the most challenging books you've read in the sense that this might be the first time you're consciously examining your deep-seated thoughts and beliefs about money, abundance, prosperity, and, possibly, scarcity. In a society where discussions about sex and our sexuality were taboo just a few short decades ago, now the new taboo is our shame and guilt relating to money. Do you have lots of it or are you in search of it? I'll warn you in advance that some uncomfortable thoughts may surface as you examine feelings and thoughts that you didn't even realize you had.

The unexamined life is not worth living.
–Socrates

I was in a very serious car accident when I was about eight years old, and was involved in a couple more during my teenage years. All were striking blows from behind.

In my early twenties, I finally had had enough of the pain and suffering and I sought out the healing comfort of an excellent chiropractor. I went in with excruciating neck pains and asked the doctor if he could help. My pain had lived with me for years and was exclusively in my neck area, day and night. It had caused headaches and even debilitating migraines almost every day during those years. I was used to the pain.

After several treatments with my new dream doctor, my body started to get stronger and I knew that I had found the path and treatment to a new and pain-free body. Feeling strong and cocky and certain that I was again invincible, I failed to book any followup appointments—until the next migraine struck, debilitating my spirit.

By the time I made it back to his office, my neck was stiff and the headaches were again with me constantly. But something strange happened after that treatment: my neck started to feel better immediately but my back, for the first time in my life, ached as it never had before. I was shocked. Why was my back pain so severe? Why had I come in to get my neck corrected only to leave with an entirely new set of problems?

I raised this concern with my chiropractor and I remember the chart that he brought out of one of the drawers in his desk. He explained that the body works on the principle of what he called a recovery of numb, pain, and normal. He also explained that the trauma of each car accident likely localized the impact and fright of the accidents in my back. Over time, I suppressed the pain in my back, which went into a numb state, and the pain was manifested as further agony in my neck, head, and jaw.

None of his explanations made sense to me at that time. Here I was going along with a body ache that I was used to—my neck. I'm leaving his office with excruciating back pain and I'm supposed to believe that I've simply been suppressing this pain and it's a good thing that I'm feeling it? Anyone who has been to a chiropractor probably knows what I'm talking about, and I'm glad to report that my back pain subsided within a few treatments and finally did clear up my neck pain.

We often focus on one thing in our body or life. It masks something more painful that we've suppressed to the point of numbness just so we don't need to relive the pain. The chiropractic form of medicine teaches us that we must sometimes bring the pain to the surface again and "feel" it so that we can move past it.

I tell you this story because you are likely to have experiences and beliefs that, once brought forward, may cause you pain. The great news is that once you're feeling the pain, you have the opportunity to move forward to a state of increased clarity and greater mental health. When these emotions are buried deep within you, no exploration or solution can be achieved. Embrace the uncomfortable feelings you might experience, and have faith and trust that a new and wonderful experience exists on the other side of this uneasiness.

> The best way out is always through.
> –Robert Frost

Do you know the difference between money and finance? It's pretty hard to tell these days as we so rarely even see or experience the feel of money in our hands any more. We pay with plastic and log into our Internet banking accounts to make sure that our paycheque was indeed directly deposited this week.

Money is what you carry in your pocket. You might use it to pay for your groceries or for dinner out this week. It's tangible and simple to comprehend and work with. The world of finance, however, seems more vague and less tangible. Think about purchasing a home for a moment. Perhaps you've done this recently or are on your way to doing so. How much would you pay for your home, $80,000, $340,000, or $800,000? Even if your home were on the low side of $80,000, try going to your local bank and requesting this money in cash for your purchase. It just doesn't happen anymore.

I remember one of my bank managers telling me that when he started many years ago, all bank managers were equipped with guns and it was common for them to help out if a competing bank ran short of funds. He told me that he would simply load up his briefcase with as much as half a million dollars in cash and deliver it himself to the bank in need. In today's world, and for so many obvious reasons, solid security companies are now equipped with the guns and the means for transporting cash.

The point here is that large amounts of cash are rarely handled today. This is true whether you're a bank manager or a customer who is ready to purchase a big-ticket item. We are now in the realm of finance. Whatever amount you decide to spend on your home, you will likely just be signing pieces of paper. Could you imagine transporting the required hundreds of thousands of dollars to the person you're buying the home from? I'm not even sure the seller would welcome it, given the world of counterfeit bills we now live in.

The larger the purchase, the more slips of paper you end up signing for this new home. What's the point? The point is that we must first understand the difference and experience the tangibility of money on the one hand and the intangibility of finance on the other.

> If you think that something small
> cannot make a difference, try going to
> sleep with a mosquito in the room.
> –Anonymous

Let's try a game based on those devised by a wonderful teacher of prosperity and abundance, Frederic Lehrman. I was grateful to learn these games from his audio program.

Imagine for a moment that I've just given you $1,000 for a game that I'd like you to play. You only need about 90 seconds of uninterrupted time to play, so find a quiet spot for a few moments.

The rules for the game and spending the money are as follows:

• You must spend the entire $1,000 on yourself.
• You must spend the money for your own pleasure and by the end of the day.
• You are not allowed to make a payment for something you'll realize in the future, pay a bill, or give it to charity.

Remember, this is just a game to see what you'd spend the money on for your *own* pleasure within a 24-hour period.

Are you ready? Now write down what ideas first came to mind:

1. _____
2. _____
3. _____
4. _____
5. _____

Were you able to spend the $1,000 quite effortlessly? Did you do it within the day? Great. Congratulations and you've won today's game.

Let's play again. Same rules; same dollar amount. Take a few moments to detail what you would purchase today and it must be something different than yesterday:

1. _____
2. _____
3. _____
4. _____
5. _____

Were you successful again? I imagine this task was still relatively effortless. Now fast forward to day three, and four, and even seven. Take a few moments to think of new ways and items that you might purchase for your pleasure, for each of those days. How about every day for thirty days? How about every day for an entire year? How do you feel about this game now?

Whenever I play this fun game during my lectures, I find, as you might have, that most participants start running out of ideas by about day seven. I have yet to experience an audience that could easily make it to week two and cetainly they are much slower at coming up with ideas. Participants report that the game isn't fun after the first week and spending the money becomes a chore, an effort.

Spending a mere $1,000 per day is not a difficult task. After all, $1,000 per day is just $365,000 per year and there are a good number of people that earn more than that as an annual salary. I've personally known friends and clients who spend more than this, on average in a year and they still manage to go about their lives without the spending becoming a consuming task.

With the advent of the Internet, I could spend $1,000 per day for my own pleasure by the time I've finished my morning coffee, and for many years, before I would ever run out of ideas, if I ever did.

So what's the purpose of the game? It's threefold. First, by chunking down an amount that most of us can relate to, we can picture what we might purchase with that money. It's likely that if you've travelled recently, you carried that much cash (i.e. traveller's cheques), if not more, on your holiday. It's a tangible amount and can be spent easily within a day or week. I want you to feel what spending that amount means to you as we so rarely use cash in our society anymore and have moved into the world of finance— just trading and signing pieces of paper.

Secondly, if you had difficulty spending the money mentally past the first week or month, you might have a problem with money or, should you amass your ideal fortune, you might not reap the benefits and luxuries that money can provide. By not consciously knowing what you would do with the $1,000 past day ten, for example, you could at some level be saying, "No, no, don't give me the money yet, I don't even know what to do with it."

Our aim here is total congruency about receiving money in our lives and reaping the pleasure that is affords us. Furthermore, if you couldn't come up with a reasonable amount of items for your spending pleasure, what's the point of pursuing more wealth? By revisiting this game and playing until you can comfortably come up with several months of spending with little to no effort, you're affirming to your subconscious that you deserve, are ready, and comfortable with spending money on yourself and for your own pleasure. We'll examine this further in chapter four with a number of fun and unique banking games.

The third and last point to this game is to identify how much you really need to feel financially secure and wealthy. Over the years, when I've asked clients or course participants how much they really need in a bank account to feel financially set, the majority in my informal polling come up with unrealistic numbers. Some have stated numbers such as several million dollars when they might be only earning five-figure incomes. When asked to play the game, if they could barely make it past week one, spending this relatively small amount of money (compared to their goal of having several million dollars), why would they feel they needed so much? You might also re-examine your financial "comfort" goal. Do you still need as much as you thought or could your goal be adjusted to a more realistic amount after playing this game? We'll explore goal setting and self-sabotaging behaviours in chapter five.

Let's play another game. You might be a bit skeptical at this point. You might be thinking that you're not quite convinced that your doubts or your old mindsets about money really have anything to do with anything. Maybe you think prosperity, abundance, and wealth are simply manifestations of luck and you've never been the lucky type. I too felt misgivings when I first studied these money principles. So if you're finding yourself in that category, this next game is really for you.

> Minds are like parachutes.
> They only function when they are open.
> –Sir James Dewar

Are you ready? You don't need a notepad or pen for this game; just read along, try it, and see what you think. Let's play!

This game requires that you dedicate just five minutes per day for thirty days. I know that you're likely to be a very busy woman as you read these pages now but I also know that everyone has five minutes free each day, for just thirty days. In this five-minute period, find a quiet spot for yourself, put on some relaxing music if you like, and totally focus all of your energy on developing a major disease…did you hear that? Spend five minutes per day, every day for thirty days imagining that you have or are developing a major disease!

Has your jaw dropped wide open? Are you ready to throw this book out the window right about now? Now, I didn't really expect you to go through with this exercise but it got your attention, didn't it? Why don't you want to spend this time visualizing the manifestation of a major illness? Why wouldn't you want to take part in this game? Everyone, hands down, that I've ever taught this game to believed the same thing: that if they truly focus their minds on developing a major disease, *it could happen*! And it could, couldn't it? Just a few minutes per day and you could turn your thoughts into something major.

> Believe your life is worth living and
> your belief will help create the fact.
> –William James

Now, what if I asked you, instead of this game, to play with the same five minutes per day for thirty days but, instead of ill health, I asked you to imagine your body to be strong and vital? What if I had told you that you could "cure" an illness or dramatically improve your energy and overall health with just five minutes per day for a month or so? What would your response have been then? If you're like the many I have taught this to, if I had started with the good-health visualization first, you would likely have just sloughed it off, claiming that "it's just too simple." That the same time and energy could produce a negative event in your body but couldn't possibly produce something positive and wonderful is the same thinking process that we use in connection with money and wealth.

Many of us think that obtaining money is hard, that creating wealth and prosperity must take great effort, that it couldn't possibly be simple and fun. If you don't believe in either version of this game, you're free to try it for yourself and see what happens. Rather than suggesting you try the "ill health" exercise, if you feel that it could work, why not try the "good health" exercise?

Thoughts Have Power

In today's day and age, a couple of viruses are commonplace if you own a computer and a body. We're inundated with attacks on our e-mail accounts and are prepared each fall for whatever new strain of flu that has migrated to our country of residence. One of the most important viruses of which you might not be aware is the dreaded thought virus. This is when a friend, family member, the media, or society as a whole makes us believe that the norm, or their interpretation of the norm, is right. It might be normal to be sick each winter with the flu or a cold but it's not right or just. Many people with strong and healthy immune systems fight off such bugs with fervor and escape such afflictions. Understanding that hackers are constantly sending out viruses, protecting yourself with a good anti-virus program is a must for your computer. But what about our minds? Can thoughts infiltrate our consciousness like a bug or Internet attack?

If you question whether or not insidious little thoughts and notions can affect the most brilliant and questioning of minds, pay close attention from now on to this widely used word: *anyways*. We often use this word several times a day as a simple bridging word or to focus our statement on a new subject. Listen and be keenly aware of how many times your radio announcer, friend, or someone e-mailing you uses this word. Have you figured out where I'm going with this yet? The correct use of this word is "anyway." There's no plural, yet this skewed use of language is common.

The deceptive nature of the thought virus is that it's often undetected. Certainly it takes someone to at least point out something like the word *anyway* being incorrectly pluralized as it did for me over a decade ago. I get a shiver up my spine when the most intelligent people make this mistake but it reminds me to question so much of my daily habits and what I hold to be true.

You've likely heard of the placebo effect. *Placebo* is Latin for "I shall please." Basically, the placebo effect occurs when a sugar pill or similar non-drug treatment is administered to a patient who is led to believe that this treatment will have a certain effect on their system. Some believe the placebo effect is psychological, caused by a belief in the treatment or to a subjective feeling of improvement. It could be a cholesterol-lowering treatment, pain relief, or remedy for an infection.

Psychologist Irving Kirsch at the University of Connecticut believes that the effectiveness of Prozac and similar drugs may be attributed almost entirely to the placebo effect. He and Guy Sapirstein analyzed nineteen clinical trials of antidepressants and concluded that the expectation of improvement, not adjustments in brain chemistry, accounted for 75% of the drugs' effectiveness. "The critical factor," writes Kirsch, "is our beliefs about what's going to happen to us. You don't have to rely on drugs to see profound transformation." (Source: Irving Kirsch. "Listening to Prozac but hearing placebo." *Prevention & Treatment*. June 1998. Vol. 1 (1) 2.)

In an earlier study, Sapirstein analyzed thirty-nine studies, conducted between 1974 and 1995, of depressed patients treated with drugs, psychotherapy, or a combination of both. He found that 50% of the drug effect is due to the placebo response. (Source: Robert Todd Carroll, *The Skeptics' Dictionary.*)

Is it mind over matter? Can an illness be learned? The placebo effect proves that thoughts do indeed have power. But why or how does one learn to have a sick mind? Think back to how you learned the English language as a child. Can you remember exactly *how* you learned? If so, learning a new language should come easy to you. The important element is awareness. Parallel the placebo effect for healing our bodies and the power of your own mind to heal *your* body. We can extend this effect to our finances as well. If we have a "sick" mind, can you see how that might spill over into the manifestation (or lack thereof) of wealth and tangible abundance in your life? Or, if money isn't the issue, an ill mind will surely keep us from the pleasure and happiness of fully enjoying our money.

The placebo effect is a profound discovery. It is perhaps one of the great studies of all time and gives us just a paltry look at the power of our thoughts to actualize our destiny, whether it includes health, wealth, bliss, or peace.

Most thought viruses effectuate themselves in words

and in many cases can actualize in our bodies or pocket books. A simple statement such as "that makes me sick" is a command to our nervous system as we will explore below. An advanced extension of this affliction is called the nocebo effect and is the real reason I wanted to introduce you to the placebo effect (if you weren't already familiar with it).

Nocebo is Latin for "I will harm." The nocebo effect is an ill result that can be caused by the suggestion or belief that something is virulent. It's only been since the 1990s that the term *nocebo* became popular; before then, both pleasant and harmful effects thought to be due to the power of suggestion where commonly referred to as being part of the placebo effect.

> I can believe anything, provided
> that it's quite incredible.
> –Oscar Wilde

So what's my point in explaining the nocebo effect? The first point is awareness; an alertness of when someone makes a statement and that person is in a position of influence or trust. Your belief in that statement may permeate your being or affect the outcome. Your normal questioning self is suppressed by an instant convincer.

Deepak Chopra discusses the nocebo effect at great length in his books and audio programs. He provides an example of a woman who's been diagnosed with breast cancer. If she totally trusts her physician, who we'll assume then tells her that 90% of the patients with this type of cancer will die, this statement could be a self-fulfilling prophecy. What about the 10% that didn't die from this type of cancer? If the doctor focused on that statistic in the prognostication, perhaps the mortality rates would totally change.

Chopra delves further into statistics citing that no matter the average annual temperature in your city, it doesn't tell you anything about what the temperature is today. And if the average income in your city is $30,000 per year, it doesn't tell me a thing about your income. The obvious point is that a prognosis is often a conclusion based on statistics and should that patient fully believe the focus of their doctor, their fate may be sealed.

> There are three kinds of lies: lies,
> damned lies, and statistics.
> –Benjamin Disraeli

What about "cold and flu season"? Every fall and winter, advertisers of cold and flu medications bombard our TV sets and radios with proclamations that these viruses are unavoidable and you will catch them. The same holds true during the spring with allergy season. What about the people who never or rarely get a cold or flu? It's not virus season for them. We must hear and become aware of the possibility of nocebos all around us and make informed decisions for ourselves.

Regarding wealth building and attracting more abundance in our life, we may be limited by the nocebos of our family, friends, and associates at work. Someone that you trust might declare that because you come from a certain background and maybe have a limited education, for example, you're destined for a mediocre existence. If you don't question this judgment or statement, you may just fulfill this decree the rest of your life. And if you hear it continually and insidiously for a long period of time, say from a parent, spouse, or friend, it may seep so far into your subconscious that it forms part of your core belief system.

Words Have Power

> High thoughts must have high language.
> –Aristophanes

Just as important as your thoughts, words too have significant power. Words, and the way we use them, form an integral part of the steps we must take on the path towards changing our beliefs about wealth and prosperity, and ultimately achieving our goals. Every time we make a statement, we are affecting our nervous system and, possibly, exposing ourselves to thought viruses. How many times have you heard or said the following sentences?

- John is filthy rich.
- Margaret is disgustingly wealthy; the way she spends so freely just makes me sick.
- Thanks for the invitation to the mountains this weekend, but it's just too rich for my blood.

Can you think of a few more? Take a moment to list three or more disempowering beliefs about money and wealth that could limit your congruency with achieving more of it:

1. _____
2. _____
3. _____

So let's take the first sentence about John being "filthy rich." Have you ever heard this one? A person describes money, or someone who has money, as filthy. Let's pretend that you've just identified that you would like to be wealthy and prosperous according to your own perceptions. What's being said in the statement about John? Basically, that it's filthy to be rich. If you're guilty of making these statements from time to time, you've been commanding your nervous system to believe that money is equivalent to filth. Now who wants to be considered "filthy" or dirty or wrong? We'll just stay poor or at our less-than-ideal state so as not to create a wrong situation. How can you ever become wealthy if it's wrong?

If you can't foster a positive view of wealthy people now (mentally, at least), especially if you're not rich, then I guess you don't want to be rich one day, right? The same is true if you think all rich people are evil or malicious or have given up something for financial gain. On the other hand, if you really wanted to be rich and thought it would be a good state to achieve, you would embrace the notion of supporting your future (rich) self.

I think you're beginning to see that there might be some internal conflict when you make a statement that would appear to be as innocent as saying "John is filthy rich" or some other derogatory comment about wealth and money. How can you not support wealth in others when this is the direction towards which your aspirations are heading? It's really as simple as knowing you have a choice—a choice to decide quickly and easily to speak and think only those words and sentences that support the image you'd like to create one day, even if that day seems far away. It's always easy to take the low road, to rationalize why some have done well for themselves while you're still perhaps several or many steps away from your goal. But taking the low road in this instance, through verbal or mental bashing, has far-reaching effects beyond the obvious integrity issues. You're sending commands to your nervous system.

I know it might be difficult for you to believe that simple thoughts and words have such great power—powers that can shape our world for the better or for the quite worse. I've always known this intuitively but my linear critical mind has always begged for scientific proof. Although no such proof to my knowledge exists, we know that there is a cause-and-effect relationship between our environment and our health. We'll discuss the power our environment has over our thoughts, our emotional well-being, and our overall health in chapter six. Perhaps our intuition is sufficient proof and scientific proof unnecessary for us to conclude that classical music is more soothing than rock music; spas have certainly figured this out long ago.

Summary

• Are you willing to be wealthy? Be willing to hear the truth as you ask yourself this question in the coming weeks.

- Keep in mind the difference between money and finance and consider how much you really need to feel wealthy.
- Are you ready to receive money and are you open to wealth? How many more ways could you spend your $1,000 per day? Stay open to receiving money by thinking how you would spend it and focus on more of it showing up in your life.

Your Prosperity Action Steps

- Complete the Self Assessment Questionnaire #2
- Write down the question, "Am I willing to be wealthy?" Listen carefully over the next day, week, or month and record your responses and self-talk.
- Play the $1,000 per day game for at least one week. List ten to twenty original items or activities that you could spend the money on and instill the concept within your subconscious that you are ready and willing to receive money now!

Chapter Three
Understanding the Laws

They are able because they think they are able.
–Virgil

The Three Laws of Prosperity

Think back to the last time you bought a car. Perhaps it was a green Toyota Camry. What happens right after you make this purchase? You usually start noticing all the green Toyota Camrys on the road and think: "Where were they all before?" I have always purchased a vehicle that, at first, I thought was quite exclusive in my city in terms of colour, make, or model. I then find, in a week or so, that there are dozens, if not hundreds of them on the road. How is that possible? How did you and I not see those vehicles before if they have always been right there in front of us?

This is called your reticular activating system and it controls a complex system of neurons in the brain stem. This system filters, relays, and regulates input between the central nervous system and the cerebral cortex. In its filtering and mediating functions, it influences those stimuli to which we respond and which we perceive as a state of immediacy. Basically, this system determines which stimuli, out of the millions we experience in a day, or even in a moment, we will focus on and pay attention to and which we will ignore or delete. (Source: Wikipedia.)

The three laws of prosperity will help you understand unconscious thoughts and behaviors that you might have never examined consciously or even realized that they resided deep within your being. These laws have been adapted from Frederic Lehrman's *Prosperity Consciousness* audio program and have been altered here in light of my own experiences and those of the many groups to which I have taught these principles.

Law #1:
What You Think About Expands

Anthony Robbins refers to human beings as "deletion creatures" and it's apparently true in my life and might be in yours as well. Basically, in any given moment of our life, no matter how simple the event might be, we have the potential to take in thousands of pictures, thoughts, sounds, or feelings. Just look around the room you're in right now. What are you focusing on? How many different things can you identify by being truly aware of your surroundings at this moment—things that you had never noticed before? We can absorb only so many stimuli in any given situation, so the rest must be deleted or not absorbed at all.

When you purchase the green Toyota Camry, your mind focuses on that type and colour of car—you see them for the first time. You might not even notice the silver Mercedes and the burgundy Yukon—they've been left out as you laser in on what you're looking for.

If you're still not sure how what you think about expands, let's try this: Don't think of the colour blue! What has just happened? You thought or pictured something blue, right? Your mind doesn't understand negatives. That's right, your mind cannot understand a negative in a command. For you to understand what not to do, in this case thinking of the colour blue, you have to think about it and then tell yourself not to think of it after you've already done so. Now, if I gave you the command, "Don't think of the colour blue" and you simply repeated to yourself, "Think of something red or green," your mind would have refocused to what you wanted it to do, not what I commanded you to do. This is a very powerful realization.

So often we tell ourselves and others "not" to do something when all the while we're actually commanding them, and ourselves, to do what we think we're avoiding. Have you ever told someone, "Don't drop that cake" and invariably the person trips or slips and drops the cake? Or,

"Don't fall" and they do? We must focus the statement when speaking to others or ourselves on the outcome that we're attempting to produce. What if we changed the previous statement to: "Walk slowly as you cross that slippery patch of ice over there"? Now that person is focused on walking slowly and cautiously, not on falling.

It works the same way in our lives: what we think about expands. How often have you told yourself not to think of something that's bothering you and you end up not sleeping all night as you try to avoid thinking about your problem? What if you tried focusing on the solution? Sheer resistance and a strong will might not work when you try to "stop thinking" about problems, they just keep seeping back into your consciousness. If you're worried about your bills, thinking about them will just expand your worries and likely create more bills. What if, instead, you thought of all the creative ways you could earn more money? What if you looked around at what you could sell, figured out a way to get that raise at work or quietly focused on the plethora of other opportunities that are just waiting for your attention?

Directing your thoughts to achieve greater control in your life is not difficult and is one of the simplest and most immediate actions you can take, right now, to change your life. It just requires patience and time. In his audio program with Wayne Dyer, *How to Get What You Really Want*, Deepak Chopra states that we think over sixty thousand thoughts a day and 95% of those thoughts are the same ones we had yesterday. Good habits and poor habits are formed; they don't happen overnight.

Manifesting Your Hero

In the early spring of 2004, just as I was entertaining writing my first book, *The Prosperity Factor*, I met my hero and it was the first time since reaching adulthood that I felt like a kid again. Unlike many of the other children I went to school with, I didn't seem to have a "hero"—other than my mother and Jesus. I had no others whom I felt it was all-important to meet. In my early twenties, I travelled a fair bit and had the opportunity to meet many celebrities. I found that they were just like you and me, with the same struggles and challenges. Their fame was based on TV or big-screen appearances and this was enough for the general public to attribute some sort of significance to meeting them. For me, it was a letdown.

In my late teens, I was blessed by happening upon, during a PBS pledge drive, a TV program featuring Dr. Wayne Dyer. This author and speaker truly changed my life. At the time, I had two part-time jobs and was finishing my schooling, so it was next to impossible to find the time for leisure reading. I visited our local library and discovered an audio book series by Dr. Dyer. I picked up one of his earlier series and listened to him every morning as I got ready for my day and each night for a few minutes as I prepared for bed.

As the years passed, I found that books on tape were one of today's greatest treasures. I discovered that I could learn and add the wisdom of great teachers to my own life without even needing to take a minute away from day-to-day activities. Whether cleaning the house or driving in the car, my audio programs were, and are always, close by.

> Nurture your mind with great thoughts;
> to believe in the heroic makes heroes.
> –Benjamin Disraeli

The most recent program by Dr. Dyer I have listened to, and the one that I continue to replay each year, is *Manifest Your Destiny*. I would highly recommend it to you. If you can't afford to buy the program or are not sure if you'd like to make the investment, although it will be some of the most rewarding money you'll spend, visit your local library and check it out for free.

Dr. Dyer's program teaches about the power of intention, whether it's finding that hammer that's been lost for years or finding the love or career of your life. His message is clear and easy: focus on your intention and watch the magic happen.

Well, the magic did happen for me one day and it is one of the great memories in my life. I smile each time I think of the coincidence of meeting my hero Dr. Wayne Dyer. If I really wanted to meet him in the past, I could have bought a ticket to one of the talks he has given in my city. I'm generally aware of the lectures that have taken place over the years, but somehow each time he was in town, I would either miss his talk or hear about it afterwards. That suited me just fine as I always preferred to allocate my funds to one of his audio programs rather than a live talk, as the tapes and CDs remain with me for later listening and study. But in my heart of hearts, I knew that I wanted to meet him one day.

During the summer of 2004, I had the unique and felicitous opportunity to finally meet one of my heroes. The words of Dr. Wayne Dyer have graced the airwaves of my home for over a decade. I've been a fan of his work, and although have never had the time to read any of his books, I have listened to everyone of his audio programs, and numerous times at that.

After the wrap-up of a conference I had attended, the last speaker of the day was one that I had attended just weeks previous and decided to head home early. I was also searching for my mother in the hotel lobby as she accompanied me on my road trip. All of the small and seemingly insignificant details and delays of the day led me to a memorable occasion. While waiting for my mother, I heard a voice that could only be that of Dr. Dyer. Of course, I knew what he looked like, but am sure I would have missed him if my ears had not been trained to pick up his voice.

Dr. Dyer actually has a book entitled *You'll See It When You Believe It* and I'm convinced that our chance meeting, filled with hugs and dialogue, was not a coincidence at all.

> Forget injuries, never forget kindness.
> –Confucius

What does your hero look like? What does your hero sound like? If Edgar Allan Poe or Albert Einstein or Ralph Waldo Emerson were still alive today and walked into the restaurant where you were eating your dinner, would you have any idea who they were? Study your heroes carefully. Put your energy into meeting them one day and, hopefully, you'll find yourself having a similar experience to mine and manifesting a great story for your children.

The 30-Day Mental Cleanse

Most health books that you pick up will certainly outline a cleansing system for maximum health and vitality. Bad eating habits and environmental toxins build up in the body and reduce its efficiency. Whether it's a juice fast or one of the many other cleanses, most experts agree that clearing out toxins will assist the body in creating a state of health and balance.

> We are what we think about all day long.
> –Ralph Waldo Emerson

Think of this next exercise as a gentle mental cleanse, along the same lines as a physical cleanse. Find an ordinary or colourful elastic band. Now, are you ready for this simple game? Put the elastic band on your left wrist, and every time you have a negative thought, give it a snap. As mentioned before, we think thousands of thoughts a day and most of those thoughts are repeats from the day before. The first step in changing an old habit is to become aware that it exists. We must first become aware of these negative thoughts about ourselves, our abilities, and the world around us. The little snap is a great reminder as these thoughts occur.

But it's not nearly enough to simply become aware of

our current patterns; we must go a step further and replace our current behaviour with more positive behaviour. Do you know someone who quit smoking (perhaps yourself) only to replace that habit with frequent snacking, thereby gaining weight and creating a new destructive pattern? What if that person had replaced smoking with exercising? How might that have changed the reformed smoker's body and experience? It's not enough to interrupt our thoughts with a "snap"—we must be ready to fill ourselves up with something better and more positive.

The first law of thermodynamics tells us that we cannot create or destroy energy, it only changes form. So what will replace your negative and self-limiting or destructive thoughts? Well, the simplest way would be to keep your mind focused on the opposite. If you find yourself worrying about your bills, you could give yourself a brief and simple snap and remind yourself to focus on new ways of earning more income. Instead of beating yourself up for that terrible sales call, you could just give yourself a snap and focus on all the ways you could have handled yourself more confidently and what you'll do differently on your next call. Instead of resenting your partner for not supporting your new business idea, you could just give yourself a snap and remember all the times you have received love and support.

> Most people are about as happy as
> they make their minds up to be.
> –Abraham Lincoln

I write these words with my sixth mental cleanse in progress. The first time I tried this exercise there was a lot of snapping going on. It also took some time to get used to wearing the elastic band and to remember to snap. I wore my elastic for forty-two days on my first round. Whether showering, dressing for an elegant evening, my elastic adorned my wrist, day and night, for forty-two days.

Whenever my family and friends asked if I had forgotten to take the elastic off after work, it gave me a great opportunity to teach them the game that I was playing with my thoughts.

The second time I was ready for another mental cleanse (just like a physical cleanse, once is never enough), I found myself snapping much less. By the third time I tried this game, I found that just looking at the elastic was enough to remind myself of my thoughts and my absolute power to change them at any time and within a moment. How freeing it is to remember that our thoughts are one of the things in life that we can truly control. We can't always control most of what happens in life; our family, friends, and workplace often take on powers of their own. But our thoughts are always within our own control.

Positive anything is better than negative nothing.
–Elbert Hubbard

The Importance of Gratitude

What if simply thinking the opposite just won't work for you in certain circumstances? Perhaps your negative thoughts concern the loss of a loved one or a job. Maybe these thoughts are simply a session of self-pity. Gratitude is the great rescuer for any pity session you can imagine. During times of negative mental loops, where you just keep replaying comments or reliving moments that no longer serve you, look around at all that you have and focus on being grateful if you can't focus on being positive. You wouldn't keep re-watching a movie that you despised—a movie filled with negativity and despair. So why do you keep playing that movie over and over in your mind? It's as simple as shifting to a spirit of gratefulness.

If you live in Canada or the United States, there are likely millions, if not billions, of people who would gladly take your place for the chance to live on "free" soil. Imagine your life without running water, a heated home, or the political freedom to criticize your government without a fear of the repercussions. If you have the gift of sight, can hear, and have fully functioning arms and legs, you are truly blessed indeed. It's often been said that if everyone threw their problems into the middle of the floor, you would gladly take your own problems back. Focus on what you're grateful for in your life and watch yourself attract more of it.

I have spent a good portion of my past being ungrateful and lacking a spirit of appreciation for what I've been blessed to receive. The result? Simple unhappiness and missing out on receiving more. When we're ungrateful for what we have, how could we possibly appreciate more? Just like the lottery winner, no matter how much we get, we'll either push it away or be unhappy with what we've been given, or worse, we won't receive more at all. The solution? Be in the present. I know this sounds simple but I've found it to be the most challenging task in my life and it continues to be so on a daily basis.

Think about children again for a moment. You just have to sit outside for a few moments with a child and within minutes they're pointing out butterflies, birds, and other treats of nature that the average adult doesn't notice. As we think of the items on our daily to-do lists or of something that happened or could happen, we're not in the present moment. Being in the here and now opens a world of opportunities that might be missed if our mind is in the past or future.

Why is it that we're often the most appreciative and grateful for that which we've lost? When a loved one is gone we think of how precious those times were. When a leg or arm is broken, we truly appreciate all that our limbs enable us to do. When we appreciate life and all that we have, we focus on the "now" and receive all of the blessings of doing so.

The last method for replacing negative thought patterns with our elastic-band exercise involves living one day as your hero. We all have conversations with ourselves in the form of self-talk. When we talk to ourselves, it's as though two different people are speaking to each other. Think of someone you greatly admire, either living or dead; someone with whom, if you had the opportunity, you would grasp at the chance of spending one day.

Now practice your self-talk and, when you do, converse only in your head and to yourself as if you were speaking to your hero. If your hero was self-reproachful about a bad speech, would you allow it? No, you'd console your hero by pointing out how great the talk was, how great previous ones had been, or that it didn't matter as there would be opportunities in the future to do better. If your hero was over for dinner and spilled red wine and lasagna all over your newly installed cream carpet, you would quickly slough it off by saying that you had a wonderful stain remover that would make it as good as new or that you could just get the carpet cleaners in to deal with it. What if you or your spouse made the same mistake? How many times would the words "clumsy, stupid, and careless" come out of your mouth or circulated in your thoughts? Treat and talk to yourself, and those important to you, as if they all are the greatest heroes on earth.

Random Acts of Kindness

There's no greater remedy for getting off of your own "pity pot" than to focus on another being. I'm sure you can recall a time when someone did something selflessly for you and for no other reason than to extend kindness and love. I was heading home from the airport one morning at about 6 a.m. and I could feel myself coming down with what was sure to be a whopper of a cold or flu. My boyfriend Wyatt was at the time leaving for Memphis on a week-long trip. It was the first time in our relationship that we were apart for any length of time. And although it was no great tragedy, I was feeling a little lost and lonely that morning.

I decided to pick up a coffee at the nearby drive-through Tim Hortons before heading to the office for work. Spaced-out while waiting for my coffee in the drive-through, I realized I was near the window and started fishing through my wallet for change. When at the window, I held out my change in exchange for the coffee and the girl smiled and said, "No charge today." I woke up out of my daze and said, "Excuse me?" She told me that the man in front of me paid for my coffee, and I looked up to see a very old and rusted van drive off into traffic and disappear forever.

> We make a living by what we get,
> we make a life by what we give.
> –Winston Churchill

As I drank my coffee on the way to the office, I realized that the kind fellow who made my day could never be thanked and obviously didn't want to be. I didn't know him and will never know who he is but he sent a spirit of cheer through me for the entire day and each time I recall the event. He certainly could have bought coffee for the person in front of him should he have wanted recognition, but he didn't.

What kind act could you extend to someone today, this week or just once each month? I've listed a few ideas and have more posted on my web site at www.thewomans-guidetomoney.com. Be sure to share your ideas and experiences so we can all bring more kindness to those that share this blue planet with us.

- **Buy Someone Coffee:** Just as in my story above, the next time you're in line at the drive-through, find out how much the person's bill behind you is, and if it's feasible and you are in a giving mood, pay their bill. If it's morning, it's more than likely that they haven't ordered more than a coffee. For less than $2, you've driven away by the time the person reaches the drive-up window and you've made their day.

- **Leave Your Quarter:** The next time you're shopping at a grocery store that requires you to insert a quarter in exchange for their buggy, leave the quarter inside. It's not much, but the surprised shopper who finds the buggy for free will be thrilled.

- **Give Money Freely:** The next time someone on the street asks you for money, give them what you have in change freely and without reservation. In chapter four, you'll learn a powerful affirmation to support such an action.

- **Send Cards in the Mail:** When was the last time you received anything other than a bill in the mail? Receiving a card is sure to bring a smile to the face of the recipient. It's simple and easy to do.

- **Send an E-Card:** Unlike traditional cards, an e-card is free and effortless. For no reason at all, send an e-card to someone different at least once a week.

- **Say Hello to a Stranger:** For me, this is more difficult than it sounds. My mom has a unique and effortless ability to say hello to any stranger, any time. If you're already good at this, keep practicing. If you're like me, it's a small risk to simply extend a smile and a genuine hello.

- **Give Gifts:** Drop by a senior's home at Christmas and take in all of the teddy bears that your children or friend's children wouldn't miss. Take them your extra canning or even re-gift the presents that you received last year and are collecting dust in your closet. Many of these individuals have no family and might rarely see a visitor.

You must give some time to your fellow man.
Even if it's a little thing, do something
for others—something for which you get
no pay but the privilege of doing it!
–Albert Schweitzer

Baby Steps to Change

An apple a day or a chocolate bar a day will make differences over time, and with longer spans of time, greater differences will occur. Do you think that simply changing your thoughts and the snap of an elastic band couldn't possibly change your life? It's an example of three degrees of separation. It might seem simple, but if you're heading on one path, from Vancouver for example, and change your course by three degrees, you probably won't end up too far from your destination if you go only three blocks. Travel ten or more miles and you'll assuredly end up further from your destination. Hop on a domestic flight and travel for five hours just three degrees off course and you are likely to end up in a different country.

Small changes make big differences and have enormous impacts over greater spans of time. The longer the journey, the more noticeable the effects of those three degrees. Why do you think that pilots are specially trained, experienced, and equipped with state-of-the-art technology to keep them on the correct course? And when they do move slightly off course because of an unexpected storm, they just keep adjusting their flight path to end up at their scheduled destination.

> Habit is habit and not to be flung
> out of the window by any man,
> but coaxed downstairs a step at a time.
> –Mark Twain

Law #2:
Whatever You Think Is the Absolute Truth Is What You Will Create

What do *you* think is the absolute truth? Since we walk around in a reality that corresponds with our beliefs, the point of this principle is simple. If you don't like what's happening in your life, you can either struggle to change the external reality or you can realize that what you're experiencing corresponds with what you believe to be true.

In his audio program *The Power of Purpose*, Les Brown states, "Wherever you find yourself in life, you made the appointment to be there." The great thing about this statement is that the steps—small or large, positive or negative—that you've taken in your life have all led you to where you are now. If *you* didn't lead yourself to where you are now, who did? Once you realize that you have made the appointment to be where you are in life, you can also make the appointment to be somewhere else in a year, five years, or ten years down the road. It all starts with what you think is possible for you. It all starts with a thought.

In *Unlimited Power*, Anthony Robbins tells the story of a concentration camp victim. Unless one was there to witness the horror of the Holocaust, it is virtually impossible to imagine. Many of those in the camp had become resigned to their fate and had given up any hope of finding a way out. But this particular prisoner asked a life-saving question when others didn't believe there was an option. He asked how people were getting out of the camp and saw that the only bodies leaving were dead bodies.

So one night when the corpses were being taken out to the large graves used for dumping bodies, this prisoner stripped down naked, hid in the vehicle that contained the bodies, and nearly died as more corpses were piled on top of him. He lay still for hours under the decaying bodies in the vehicle and among them when they were dumped. As soon as he knew the soldiers had left, he ran naked many miles to his freedom.

The prisoner asked a life-changing question. His reality, which he held to be true for him, was that there *must* be a way. He asked a better question and therefore was able to find a solution.

Many years ago, I decided to strike the word *impossible* from my vocabulary (perhaps because of my love of math and physics classes at an early age). I realized that advances had been made in the world, making things possible that a little earlier were said to be impossible and often were still stated as such in our textbooks.

Who knows enough to know what's possible or not? I believe that all is possible; I just might not have all of the answers—*yet*. But by believing anything is possible, I'm apt, at least, to ask the question of how a task might be accomplished, as opposed to simply resigning myself to the fact of its impossibility. If we're too stubborn, we might never know when to move on when projects are too difficult or just not worth our time. But how many people have never started a project because they believed in the notion of impossibility? How many people believed at one time that the world was flat, that flying and driving machines were illusions for the insane, or that we are moving at dizzying speeds through the universe despite the fact we seem stationary when we sit or stand? Try to see if simply deleting the word *impossible* from your vocabulary works as well for you as it has for me and so many others.

Look at your life. What thoughts of yours have created your reality? We must first change our *internal* beliefs before our *external* realities can be affected. Our beliefs literally reflect our realities. If you want to know what you've been thinking of yourself, just look at yourself realistically. You might be making excuses for what you've created but there are thousands of examples of immigrants who came to Canada and the United States, who didn't speak our language, who didn't have any friends or family to help them along and yet have become millionaires. They knew how to condition their thoughts. They knew the power of gratitude and never took one minute of living in a free country for granted. Their truths, their beliefs manifested into their reality.

> I have always thought the actions of men
> the best interpreters of their thoughts.
> –John Locke

Unconscious thinking leads to a result, and a life, we didn't intend because we didn't consciously manifest and create it. We just let life and our social, religious, and/or other peer groups lead us along. And the sad part is, we did it willingly. We bought into the social conditioning that wants us to stick close to these groups.

My pastor John Hagee tells a great story that I'd like to share with you. There's a young married couple and the wife is making dinner for her husband. She has decided to cook a ham for the evening's supper and as she prepares it, she cuts the ham in half. Her husband is perplexed by this action and asks his new wife why she cuts the ham in half before roasting it. She replies, "Well, ask my mother; that's how she taught me to cook a ham."

Later that month, the couple has dinner at the wife's parents' home and the groom finds the opportunity to ask his mother-in-law about his wife's unusual cooking ritual. When he asks the mother why her daughter cuts the ham in half, she simply replies, "When I was first married, we couldn't afford a large roasting pan and I had to cut the ham in half so it would fit in the small roaster."

The young bride had never questioned whether her style of cooking was still appropriate for the times or if it was needed, given the availability of new and inexpensive roasting pans. At some unconscious level, she had followed the lead of her mother and had never questioned or thought the process through.

How many of us are unconsciously "cutting our ham" to meet the needs of our parents or a perceived societal belief?

> Get your facts first, and then you can
> distort them as much as you please.
> –Mark Twain

Law #3:
A Thought Is Eternal
Until It Is Unthought or Rethought

This law states that all of the thoughts that you've had from the past are continuing to produce a reality, regardless of whether or not you are giving them any attention. Maybe you're in Toronto right now but you live in Vancouver and own a home in West Vancouver. Just because you're in Toronto, it doesn't mean that your home doesn't exist in Vancouver. Actually, the notion sounds silly doesn't it? But just because we're thinking a new thought, it doesn't mean that our old thoughts cease to exist.

It's like having a hold button on your subconscious. You can keep this thought on the line indefinitely and it won't hang up on you. Our memories and subconscious keep a perfect photographic reproduction of everything that has happened to us. It is the organizing of our physical reality and the maintaining of it (based on old thoughts and beliefs) that are important.

Let's explore two examples provided by Frederic Lehrman of how old thoughts continue to function even when we pay no attention to them.

Example #1: Don't take things from strangers (i.e. money, candy, etc.)

Does this sound familiar? I'm sure you'll agree that almost everyone has heard this statement before. This means that within our subconscious, and within our collective social subconscious, there is this belief that warns us not to take something from a stranger for any reason.

Example #2: If you do a favour for a friend and the friend tries to pay you, you shouldn't accept any financial reward for doing that favour.

Let's say you helped a friend paint her garage. You do this because you're friends and this is what friends do. And then one day, she discovers that she's short on funds and asks if you'd help her cover a bill until she receives her next paycheque, so you do so. And then she needs to move from her current residence to a new home and you agree to give a day of your time to help her. Finally, one day you call her and ask her to babysit. You know that your friend has no prior engagement but she gives you some excuse about how busy she is in order to get out of fulfilling your request. How do you feel about this? Doesn't she owe you for all the favours that you did for her?

This is where a "clearing of accounts" becomes so important. If, at the end of helping your friend paint the garage and after all the other favours you had performed for her, she had cleared accounts by taking you out to dinner, buying you something she knew you would like, or, if that wasn't convenient, had simply paid you money, she would have cleared the account. If this was the case before you called her to babysit, regardless of whether she was free or not, you would no longer feel "owed." All your gifts of service would have been "squared off," so even if she had said no to your request, there would not be any hurt feelings.

Back in the more elegant times of the eighteenth, nineteenth, and early twentieth centuries, rich in rituals and courtesies, society often expected a clearing of accounts of sorts. It was socially acceptable, and expected, for a grandchild to mail a handwritten thank-you note after receiving a gift or for guests at a friend's dinner party to do the same. Today, you rarely find such formal expression of gratitude and a debt of sorts therefore exists that is later to be repaid.

Returning to the example of the friend, I'm sure you'll agree that there's an underlying assumption and underlying ethic that says not to take money from your friends. That is why they're your friends, right? Lehrman tells us that two thoughts have been in the back of our mind for quite some time. Thoughts we didn't even realize were there but which alter the way we accept and spend money from others. These thoughts are:

- don't take money from strangers, and
- don't take money from friends

To understand the way our minds work, Lehrman likens it to the most fantastic supercomputer on earth and how fascinating it is at perceiving reality.

To illustrate how fast the mind works when you deal with or draw on all of your past experiences to interpret what's happening at the present moment, I'm going to relate to you a situation that I originally learned from Lehrman's *Prosperity Consciousness*. Try the following: Visualize yourself as a store owner and imagine you're sitting behind your cash register. You see something moving...what is it? Is it an elephant? No. Is it a car? No. It's...it's...yes, it's a person. This person is shopping around your store and finally chooses an item and approaches you at the cash register. He starts to pull something out of his pocket and you see something green in his hand. What is it? Is it broccoli? Is it grass? No, it's...money!

This example might seem a little absurd to you, but as events happen, your brain, like a supercomputer, searches through all of the files that it has—in this instance, on dealing with people and with money. Now your brain must search specifically for money and people as this customer hands the money to you. Your brain searches and says, "Well, this person isn't a friend and he's been in my store for quite some time now, so he can't be a stranger; therefore, he must be an enemy." Remember that logic isn't at play here. Your mind is processing this so quickly that you are rarely aware of what's happening. But how many times have you given someone money, whether to a friend, stranger, or potential enemy, and felt something wrong was going on, or something not quite right? How many times have you accepted payment for a product or a service and felt you were not completely deserving of the money, even if it was at some very small level of discomfort?

I remember the first real career job I held at a financial planning firm. I loved my new job and adored my boss and colleagues. This was a small firm, so when the first payday arrived, I knew that each dollar paid to me came either out of my boss' profits or from the potential raises of all the others who worked at the firm. Furthermore, I was having so much fun and receiving so much enjoyment from my time in this new position that it seemed more like time devoted to play rather than to work. I remember receiving that cheque and the money as if it were something shameful or wrong. It seemed wrong to me that this person, my boss, whom I admired greatly and thought of as a friend, was giving me money.

Can you relate to my story of receiving my first paycheque? Can you relate to an experience of getting or giving money that felt tainted, uncomfortable, or, perhaps, even unethical?

How do we combat these feelings of ill will towards money? How can we attract more money into our lives if we can't joyfully give and receive money for the good that it buys? Certainly, the first step is awareness. Monitor your buying and spending and see if any of these old thoughts hold true for you. Second, try the following game as practice for developing new spending and receiving habits that will help you see the good that money produces.

> The beginning is the most
> important part of the work.
> –Plato

The Economy Game

Here is another game taught by Frederic Lehrman. Find a few friends with whom you can play this game. The rules are simple. Each of you creates a list of ten items, or more, that you have given away to each other in the past for no payment and now will charge each other for under the pretext of happily giving and receiving money from friends. Keep the products or services simple and have items that range from a dollar or two up to whatever amount you would like. Remember to ensure that you're charging a fair price. By this I'm not assuming that you'll overcharge but rather that you are likely to undercharge for your product or service. Make sure you're at least getting your cost back and factor in a bit of a profit. Have fun with the game and feel free to set up a sample market at your home where your friends can bring in their products for sale and discuss the benefits of the various items. Make sure you exchange cash and do it with a smile. Thank your "customers" with a verbal acknowledgement and have all of your friends do the same.

With the prevalence of e-mail, this game becomes even easier to play. Payment can be made through the mail, which will reinforce the element of surprise when you receive the money unexpectedly. Although it is not recommended that you send cash through the mail, most would agree that $5 or $10 presents no great risk, given the benefit it will provide to the person you're sending it to. Make sure that once you've received the money in the mail, you contact your buyer cheerfully and acknowledge and sincerely thank that person for sending payment for your service. You'll enjoy the spending and receiving process and will banish from your mind the old thought that it is not okay to receive money from your friends.

A sample list of products or services could include:
- babysitting
- homemade cards, candles, gift baskets
- selling of make-up and perfume samples
- proofreading or writing of Christmas cards
- coaching
- daily inspirational quotes via e-mail

The list could go on. Each time you perform a service or give a product to a friend or receive one in return, explain this game and ask if they'd be willing to exchange money as part of playing the game. You'll always have clear accounts with your friends and will enjoy the process of helping each other gain pleasure from the giving and receiving of money.

How comfortable do you feel about giving to and receiving money from strangers? Send me your list of items and check my web site at www.thewomansguide tomoney.com for my own "mini-economy." I'll post as many items as you like and every person who reads this book can participate in this economy. Pick the products or services that you would like to purchase and spread the wealth and new money habits as you play this online game.

These games may seem simple but they have profound effects. Whether you're a salaried employee or a bona fide salesperson, you always have something to sell. Why not get comfortable with the process and condition your sub-conscious with positive experiences for greater prosperity and abundance? If you're a salesperson or business owner, you must be comfortable with receiving money or raising your prices. But even as a salaried employee, the fact that you are comfortable with your worth will give you the self-esteem you require to ask your boss for that raise you deserve.

Start now. Play the game with your friends and family and start clearing your accounts for greater relationships and ease when using money. Visit www.thewomans-guidetomoney.com to play with strangers as well. Happy spending and receiving!

> If you would thoroughly know
> anything, teach it to others.
> –Tryon Edwards

Summary

- What you think about expands. Focus on what you want and use the 30-day challenge to direct your thoughts.
- Making big changes in your life starts with baby steps. Even the smallest changes will make profound differences in your life over time. Choose healthy and prosperous baby steps.
- Whatever you think is the absolute truth is what you will create. Focus your energy internally and the external will manifest your new thoughts and beliefs.
- A thought is eternal until it is rethought. Start playing the economy game to change the way you relate to your friends and money. Play the economy game online at www.thewomansguidetomoney.com to play it with strangers and win.

Your Prosperity Action Steps

Did you find an elastic band yet? Start your mental cleanse immediately. This is a simple, fun, and extremely powerful action step.

- At the end of your day, write down three things that you are grateful for.
- In the morning, today and every day, write down three things that you would like to focus your attention on. It could be on getting a raise, finding the perfect mate, attracting a new job, living in a state of perfect health—whatever you desire. When you snap your elastic, focus on these qualities that you wish to attract into your life.
- Add some kindness to someone's life today. Try an act of random kindness from my list, check out my web site for more ideas at www.thewomansguidetomoney.com and try something new each week. Remember to e-mail me your ideas so all of us can creatively impact the world with our kindness.

- E-mail your friends about the economy game. Give them a list of your ideas and encourage them to play with you. You might consider teaching this chapter to your friends and explain the game in its entirety. That way, you benefit from teaching the material, developing your positive support group and they gain by learning a simple but powerful game.

Chapter Four
The Bank – Your Saviour?

A banker is a fellow who lends you
his umbrella when the sun is shining, but
wants it back the minute it begins to rain.
–Mark Twain

Redefining the Way You Bank

Are you complaining about your *own* profits? People have strange beliefs about banks. Many Canadians have made it their favourite pastime to complain about the success and profits of the major banks in this country. Someone forgot to tell them that they're complaining about their own success and profits—how silly is that? If you're one of the many who falls into this "I hate the banks" category, let me enlighten you about the fact that it means you hate yourself and your fellow neighbours—literally!

With the advent of mutual funds and their overwhelming popularity over the last couple of decades, it is highly probable that you own a portion of one or more of our Canadian banks. If you own a Canadian mutual fund, you likely own a portion of our country's banking system. So when you complain about "their" profits, you're really complaining about your own profits. Furthermore, we receive a lot of our news and information about the economy from the U.S. media and, although our economy often mirrors that of the States, we shouldn't compare our banking system to theirs. In our country, strict rules in Canada's *Bank Act* prevent a person or a corporation from owning a majority of the bank itself—not so in the United States. In Canada, people own the banks and yet we complain bitterly about their profits and that we are, in some way, being swindled when "they" do well.

We need only look past the six o'clock American or

Canadian news to realize and remember that when a banking system is *not* doing well, neither is the country as a whole. How quickly we forget what Japan went through just a few short years ago.

If you dislike the banks so much and resent the profit they make from allowing you to use *your* money, then stop using them and the convenience they bring to your life. Stop using that credit card and bank card at every store you frequent; don't take cash out at your local ATM at 2 a.m. on a Saturday night—after all, why should you pay to get your own money, right?

In this day and age, it's almost impossible not to use a bank unless you're paid in cash. Try using the banking system less if you feel that it's such a rip-off to pay for the convenience of paying bills online 24 hours a day. It takes people to run a bank, just as it takes people to run all the other companies in this great economy. Companies pay rent and utilities, business taxes, and the salaries of the thousands they employ. If anyone is directly to blame for the banks' desire to improve their bottom line and increase the always-criticized bank fees, blame the shareholders and their constant demand for higher stock prices and dividend payouts—again, that's likely to include you, your family and your friends.

So remember at your next family gathering to question the holders of stocks and mutual funds about their greediness and the desire for their stock or mutual fund portfolios to rise every year. Do this before you grumble at your friendly bank teller.

> If you owe the bank $100, that's
> your problem. If you owe the bank
> $100 million, that's the bank's problem
> –Jean Paul Getty

Now that I've stepped off my soapbox for the moment, I should add that as a society we hold unusual beliefs about banks and what they can do for us. We often have our pay-cheque spent before we even receive it and, should we indulge in some pleasure-filled spending spree, we feel guilt and shame. There's something wrong with our thinking that money and the bank as intermediary are bad for us!

Before we move forward, let's step back in time in order to appreciate the convenience that money, as a form of currency, has added to our way of life. Sometime in our early history as a people we had more of some product or service than we and our families needed. At the end of the season, for example, a farmer might determine that he has more than enough wheat from the harvest to last his family throughout the entire winter, and even into spring. He would then tell his neighbours about this abundance and might find that they too have an excess—but of cattle, not wheat. So, in exchange for the beef, which he needed, the farmer could trade wheat.

If there was still excess wheat from an abundant crop, the farmer could then travel further down the road seeking to sell his wares. The farmer might happen upon another neighbour who possesses a highly valued service. One, for example, has a unique tool that could till the wheat farmer's land and prepare it for winter and spring much more easily than he was able to on his own. But by using this tool, this neighbour too has an abundant crop and does not need any extra wheat. He does, however, need to secure the services of the town doctor as he has fourteen children and five of his girls are now grown and are expecting to give birth this year. He tells the farmer that if he can prepay for the doctor's services, he'll be happy to secure his special tilling tool for the fall.

In speaking with the doctor, the wheat farmer finds out that he's been paid for years with wheat and has enough in storage to last for many years. He is, however, running low on beef. The farmer agrees to obtain a supply of beef for the doctor in order to secure medical services for his neighbour who, in turn, will provide the tools and labour he needs to till his fields. It all sounds complex and exhausting, but these exchanges must take place.

What if there was a simpler way? What if the farmer had a medium of exchange—something constant—that he could receive for the abundance that his work produced and that he could use to procure someone else's abundance? Well, there is, and we shall call it *money*!

My story is fictitious; I'm not even trying to create an accurate account of the first exchanges of our time. But at the very least, this story conveys the difficulties our ancestors faced in order to trade goods and services with each other before money or currency of some type was introduced. It doesn't matter that at one time this currency was gold, at another time it was salt, and now it is paper notes and metal coins; currency is as valuable as each society determines it to be. Try using salt the next time you want to buy a sofa—funny, yes, but at one time this was the most precious commodity on earth and that's why it was used as a currency. We often hear the same thing about money; it's worthless paper, after all. A $1,000 bill is made of similar fibres and ink as a $5 bill, yet each represents a very different spending potential.

How wonderful and lovely money becomes when we remember that it is simply, and always has been, a *medium* for the exchange of goods and services. There's nothing to hate or love in the money itself. It's just fibres and ink or stamped metal. *We desire what the money buys*, the economy it runs, the life we build by securing the products and services we desire. But we also appreciate its convenience because if it weren't for money as a currency of exchange, we would spend our days creating an economy of our own by selling our excess to buy someone else's.

Now that we have an appreciation for the spending and buying process, we're ready to play! I'd like to introduce you to a game—a fun and exciting way of dealing with money. Play the game for as long or as short a time as you like but I strongly encourage you to at least get into the game. I plan to outline a very simple process for training your conscious and subconscious mind to save and spend money in a new and healthy way that will attract more of it into your life.

Before we start to play, let's look at many of the negatives that have been imposed on us by language through our use of words such as "savings account" and "emergency account" and what we're saying to our subconscious when we use these words.

Saving Yourself from the Banks:
The Five Bank Account System

Now that we have the understanding that money is simply a medium—a convenient method of exchange for acquiring the goods and services that will bring joy, abundance, freedom, and health to ourselves and our loved ones—we can shift to those ends that money facilitates. Instead of making rounds to our neighbours, as in my previous example, hoping that we have what they want and vice versa, we can use this simple medium to go out and buy specifically *what we want, when we want*.

Now, if you don't like using money, you're certainly welcome to try the old-fashioned method. Find a product or service and try to create your own economy. Many people do this on what's called a barter exchange network and enjoy the process immensely. For those of us, however, who do not have the time or inclination to barter our products and services the old-fashioned way, we need to figure out a simple means of accounting for the money that flows in and out of our lives. We need to have greater power and control over money and, with the magic of manifestation, attract more of it into our lives.

> Habit is either the best of servants
> or the worst of masters.
> –Nathaniel Emmons

From Piggy Banks to Emergency Accounts

Do you remember when money was fun? Do you remember having a piggy bank or a secret stash, knowing that those coins and colourful pieces of paper could buy you the toys and candies of your dreams, therefore making your life happy and fulfilled? There still lives inside all of us that little child who knows that money can be fun. I remember as a child the excitement I would feel when someone gave me money. I also remember that I cherished bills greatly over coins. Even at an early age, I knew that bills bought more "stuff" than coins did.

During my childhood, I had a very special Uncle Alex whom I saw only occasionally on outings with my mother. But when I did see him, and it didn't matter if several years had passed or just a few months, he would always give me a $50 bill. I rarely saw a $50 bill and I just loved its burnt orange/red colour. Later, I developed an unusual habit and affinity for this gift and ritual from my uncle, which I'll elaborate on in a moment.

I also loved the ritual of going to the bank with my mother as part of her weekly cheque-cashing and depositing routine. She would always ask for "fresh" bills because the money was cleaner if it hadn't been used or creased. I also adopted this preference from my mother and always insisted on my money appearing clean, even if it were the most tattered and torn bill in circulation. One of my favourite memories as a child was sitting on the basement stairs watching my mom and chatting with her about life as she spent hours ironing our clothes. I'd watch her meticulously spray-starching and ironing out every wrinkle so that our clothes would not only *be* clean but would also *look* particularly clean and fresh.

I was one of the few children I knew growing up who didn't like to use a piggy bank. I found the process of folding and cramming bills into this little hole disrespectful and bizarre. Furthermore, I wouldn't know how much I had saved up. When the family member who had bought me the piggy bank convinced me to use it, I found myself emptying it frequently so I could regularly count my savings.

My admiration and respect for my mother led to an interesting exercise that I used to perform on a weekly and sometimes daily basis. When my mother had finished her ironing, I would sneak back downstairs, get out the spray starch, and spray the heck out of my new dollar bills, especially those rare and very special $50 bills from my uncle. I would methodically run the iron back and forth over the bill until it reached the desired crispness. I loved the sound of the sizzle when the hot iron reached the cool spray starch and the smell of the steam and money. It felt good, and every fibre of my being was in harmony with the playful nature of the money along with my joy in what my bills would buy. So what happened to my playful childlike nature when it came to money?

I'm sure, if you think on the subject for a while, you had many fun games and tricks when it came to money. My brother and I used to find money, sometimes as much as a $10 or $20 bill on the floor of shopping malls or on the street. We were on the hunt for money and always used to compare to see who found the most. Now, in adulthood, I rarely find money but I'm not looking for it on the floor. When I do take the time to look around, as I did when I was a kid, a quarter, loonie, or more will magically show up. Somehow though, in the midst of lofty goals and high-priced toys, my enthusiasm for a quarter has waned over time. What games do you look forward to with your money? Or is money just a means to an end that you'd rather not discuss?

Now let's fast-forward to adulthood. Generally speaking, most adults have three types of bank accounts: a chequing account, a savings account, and an emergency account. Let's focus on the last one for a moment.

Almost every financial advisor you meet with or financial planning book you pick up will always insist on that all-important *emergency account*. We're told to forget about starting any type of savings account until this account has been created. Once you've passed the test of saving at least three to six months of salary in this account, you graduate to the savings account—so we're taught. First put your money away for an emergency and then put the rest of your money away until it's needed later to "save" you. What doesn't make sense here? If we know that what we focus on expands and that words have power, the prospect of an emergency and the purpose of our money one day saving us doesn't seem to be congruent—or even appealing to me.

Let's think this out logically for a minute. When you were a child, you likely had a piggy bank; that equalled pleasure. Filling the piggy bank usually followed some predetermined or even spontaneous emptying of the piggy bank (that's why there's usually a hole with an easy-to-pull-out rubber plug at the bottom) in order to buy something fun, exciting and likely just for you. This wasn't money to run the household or to pay your family's bills. Usually, the accumulation was so small that your parents or other adults gave no thought as to how the money was to be spent. So when you were a child, spending equalled pleasure.

Now trade in the piggy bank for an emergency account. What do most of us imagine when we hear the word *emergency?* You probably would think of an ambulance, as most of us do. Why are ambulances summoned? Usually because of some dreadful event. And how do they sound? They often startle us as they pass by on the street or jolt us out of a relaxing talk with a friend as we sip cocktails on a patio. So we trade in the picture of the happy, often pink and cute piggy bank we had as a child and settle, as adults, for a screaming doom-and-gloom vehicle like an ambulance. How satisfying can the creation of that type of an account be? Wouldn't *you* prefer a more elegant solution for the complexities of setting the stage for your prosperity consciousness, whether saving or spending?

Your Five Bank Account System Explained

One of the simplest ways to wealth, abundance, and prosperity has been taught by many and yet followed by very few. Frederic Lehrman, Phil Laut, and Leonard Orr have all taught the principles related to the creating of multiple bank accounts. To refine these teachings, I have used my own experience and the experiences of workshop participants and the thousands to whom I have lectured. I now bring these to you in a tested and workable format. My alterations to the various bank account systems out there arise from my own reasoning and experiments and the feedback that I have received from those to whom I have taught this system. There's no right or wrong in this game and nothing complex for you to focus on. If a particular account doesn't work for you, drop it. If you'd prefer to give it a different name from the one I've suggested or to play with an additional account, go ahead. The rule is that you start now, and be sure to have a great deal of fun!

Regardless of whether you read these pages as a thirty-nine-year-old or as a ninety-three-year-old, there is no doubt that a fair amount of money has flowed in and out of your life. The question is, if you had saved 10% of that money and lived off the remaining 90%, could you have made it? Would you have died doing so? It's almost certain that, somehow, you would have made it as easily on 90% as you would have on 100%. Why is it so easy to admit this in hindsight but not follow it in the present? Every single person I have put this question to has agreed, resoundingly, that it would not have been impossible to have lived on a little less. Yet all agree that they were never diligent about keeping to this rule. And no matter whether the person is struggling financially or has an excessive income, it seems to be a difficult task for all of us to save this little extra that makes all the difference.

The reasons for not saving range from a lack of awareness about what we are spending to sheer forgetfulness or the pressing need to pay the bills before we take care of ourselves. Most of those whom I question about their lack of savings agree that they always somehow manage to pay their bills—even the unexpected ones. If their rent increases or little Johnny just has to have new glasses, they somehow find the extra money. Interesting. We find the extra money, like magic, when we focus on the need to create it. In the case of the increased rent, most of us would agree that this is an unwelcome use of our cash flow but if you can find the extra money when a bill collector demands it, you can assuredly come up with the money for fun and creative uses also.

I know that some people can barely pay their bills each month, although somehow they manage to do it. However, they might be saying: "One day when I make more money, I'll be sure to save some if..." Listen, if we can't save when it's difficult to, we likely won't when it's easy either. It doesn't seem to matter how much our salary increases, we just find more things to spend the money on. If you have cable television and a cell phone, as most people in our society do, you're likely spending approximately $1,200 per year on just those two expenses. Could you live without cable television and your cell phone? Sure you could; the cell phone is an extremely new invention and we somehow managed thousands of years without them, and cable television is most certainly a luxury.

I'm not suggesting that you get rid of either service, but if you don't think you have enough money to save, think about what you're currently spending your funds on. Would you prefer in five years to have an extra $6,000 lying around or would you prefer to have kept watching your diurnal television shows and chatting on your cell phone? It's your choice. I know so many people who have quit smoking, and for many good reasons, but many of them quit primarily because it was too expensive. They told me that with all the money they were spending on smoking every day they assuredly could have taken several first-class vacations instead.

Now ideally it's good to quit such a bad habit, no matter what the reason, but often when I catch up with these individuals later and congratulate them after learning that they've been smoke-free for months, or years, I ask them how their savings plan is going. They all say, "What savings plan?" with a blank look on their faces. I then remind them of all the money they were going to save instead of spending it on cigarettes. I have never come across one person who saved those funds with the same diligence that went into the purchase of cigarettes. A smoking addiction and the pain of being out of cigarettes was great enough to get even the laziest of my friends out of a warm home on a -40°C winter evening. Why aren't they as driven with the same determination to leave their warm homes on an utterly freezing night to transfer funds from their general account to their savings account, all the while keeping a picture of their beach vacation in mind?

So if your excuse for not saving is that you're waiting for the day that your income increases or your expenses decrease, I have news for you: it will never happen! I have a few clients who consistently earn an average salary of about a million dollars per year after having at one time earned less than $50,000 per year and they still don't have any money left at the end of the pay period. The trick is to pay yourself first and to set that process in stone, just as if you were paying a bill. How many of us don't make our mortgage payments? Not many. Somehow, no matter how many extra expenses come up each month, we always manage to find a way to pay the bills—but rarely ourselves. So make a regular payment to yourself one of your bills. If we always find a way to pay our bills, doesn't it make sense that this method would force the 10% savings rate on us, making us as diligent about paying ourselves as we are about paying our bills?

And a quick note on paying your bills: enjoy paying them! Yes, that's exactly what I said, enjoy paying your bills. Do you hate paying bills? Do you feel resentment or a lack of enthusiasm when using your money to pay for the goods and services you receive each month? If so, you're hindering your own prosperity consciousness. People and families lie behind those bills. The gas and electricity that comes into your home each month warms you in the winter, dries your clothes within minutes, and allows you to cook meals without a thought. When you pay your utility bills, you're supporting the hundreds of employees who work at these companies, along with their families who rely on that paycheque for food, clothing, and shelter. *Your bill is their prosperity*. Bills are for the benefit of us all.

What if there was a way to support the child within each of us that would make money and the exercise of spending and saving fun again?

Bank Account #1:
My Income Account

> We are what we repeatedly do.
> –Aristotle

The purpose of the *income account* is to keep track of how much money you're actually earning. Regardless of the source of the income flowing into your life (salary, bonuses, inheritances), the rule of this account is to deposit all funds into this account first. This makes a great deal of sense for a couple of reasons. First, as we have discussed previously, we often feel that our money is spent even before we receive it. The act of depositing all of our income into this account provides a cooling-down period. This account will create a margin of time that allows you to think *before* the money is spent. The bills will still be paid, the groceries will still be bought, but *everything* must first flow through this account.

The second advantage of this account is that it provides an excellent income statement at tax time because it lists all of the income you earned in the year. It also allows you to review the amount of money that flowed into your life within the year. How much more it seems at the end of the year than it did as you were receiving it!

You will now take 10% directly off the top and allocate it to the remaining four accounts that are detailed next. The remaining 90% will go to all of the spending that you would normally do within a given month—gas, housing, food, and clothing—just as you did before. Another way to look at it is if I were to ask: if your employer had to cut your pay by 10%, could you still make it? Would you be out on the streets, destitute and starving? No, of course you wouldn't. Actually, you are likely to find it easier to manage than you ever imagined. So spend the rest of your income as you would normally, and just pay that "You" bill first in the amount of 10%.

It might seem as though it would take extra time to start playing with a bunch of bank accounts, but I assure you that they will simplify your life and make you richer, and you will better enjoy the process of saving and spending.

To recap, you're going to take 10% as a minimum and set it aside in your mind. Then we'll learn how to distribute this amount between the remaining four accounts. The 10% you're going to move from the Income account to the other accounts is your new surplus money. It's money that you should have kept but which you previously let slip through your hands. Just take a minute and roughly estimate what you have earned from all sources over your lifetime thus far. Measure 10% of it and I'm sure you'll be shocked at how much wealth you could have amassed by now.

Now that you understand the income account and the principle of setting aside 10%, I can now teach you how to divide the funds between the four other accounts.

Bank Account #2:
My Financial Independence Account
Money can serve us in many ways or it can be perceived as a forced enslavement in the pursuit of reaching

your financial goals. If the latter has been your financial path, would you like to be freed of this slavery? Wouldn't you love to live a life of independence, joy, and effortlessness where money is never again a worry? The *financial independence account* will do this for you in time but I'll warn you in advance: this account is likely to start out as your least favourite account. But after a couple of months of playing, it might very well become your most enjoyable.

The rule is, any money you deposit into this account will never be withdrawn for any reason, *ever*! It will be there for an eternity. Now I know what you're thinking: "Put a portion of my money away for an eternity and never spend it—are you kidding?" But there's more to it than that.

Let's first explore the meaning of *financial independence*. What does it mean? It means having an income that is sufficient for you to live on forever, whether you work and earn an income or not. Let's say that you currently earn $38,000 per year. Now let's say that you had the freedom to never work again, if that is what you really wanted. If this is the case, you would have to pare down your expenses a notch. What would you really need to live on? You might say $25,000; after all, many of your expenses might have been work related, such as gas and other costs related to the use of your car, dry cleaning for your work clothes, and so on. So if all you really need is $25,000 annually and you don't want to work again, let's examine the amount earning interest in a bank account that you would need in order to have this freedom.

If you had $250,000 in a bank account earning interest at a rate of 10% per year, that's $25,000 per year in interest. Therefore, all you would need in the bank is $250,000 and the interest would keep you living at that level for eternity, as long as you earned the steady 10% annual interest. For many of us, that's not a completely unimaginable amount of money to have in the bank. Let's just pretend that those numbers apply to your specific situation and every time you deposit money into your income account, you focus on the $250,000 amount.

What numbers would work for your financial independence account? How much would you need in the account with today's interest rates (which are nowhere near 10%) to generate an income that would be sufficient for you not to *need* to work again?

Remember that many people are very resistant to the idea of this account. First, they've never really imagined themselves as being financially independent, not even at retirement. Second, they resent the fact that the money in this account will never be spent. However, the interest will be spent and for very specific purposes. Spending the interest periodically is part of playing the game. And remember, this is a game. It's meant to appeal to the child within us, the subconscious. If our negative and joyless notions about money reside deep within our subconscious, we need to appeal to that deep level with creative games in order to change our old patterns and thoughts over time.

So what do we do with the interest and when do we spend it? Depending on how much you're depositing into this account, you may do either of the following:

- Determine set dates for spending this money, such as every month or every other month, or
- Wait until it's accumulated to a certain amount, say $50.

I prefer the first option as it also gets you into the habit of playing interactively at regular intervals.

The fun begins when it comes to spending the interest, which might actually turn this account into your favourite account. Take the amount of interest you made for the month, $14.02, for example, and it is very important that you use cash for this exercise. During the time that your $14.02 is accumulating, start jotting down how it might feel to be financially independent. Imagine how your surroundings would look. What would you do in the morning if you had no *need* to go to work that morning—or any morning? If you're like me, you probably have a number of books or magazines that you rarely have the time to look at. You might rush through the newspaper each morning and wish you had the time to enjoy your coffee and peruse world events at your leisure, so try this assignment: go to a coffee shop in your area or to a venue that looks and feels good, one that feels prosperous as well. You might find the lobby of one of your finer hotels provides an ideal spot. Take along your reading material and order your coffee, perhaps even a breakfast.

What would you do if you really were financially independent? Take a few minutes to detail just five things that you either don't have the time or money for but that, *when* you are financially independent, you would do immediately.

1. _____
2. _____
3. _____
4. _____
5. _____

The first thing to realize is that you'll be paying for these activities entirely from the interest of your financial independence account. You didn't have to do anything for the interest except invest it intelligently, and now you're enjoying this time because of it. Feel, look, talk, and daydream as if you are someone who is *truly* financially independent. Remember that this is a game and your subconscious doesn't know the difference between an experience that has actually happened and one that is vividly imagined. So have fun and truly experience this new notion of freedom, even if it's only for a couple of hours on a Saturday morning or a Thursday evening. An important note to keep in mind: you may not go over the amount that you have predetermined you are able to spend on this exercise. And if you're finished your breakfast and find you have a few coins left over, you might wish to redeposit them into your account. This way, you'll have even more to spend the next time you want to play.

While playing this game, you're teaching your subconscious mind, at a very basic level, that "money is fun." If you replace your old thoughts with the knowledge that money is fun and can create freedom and independence, don't you think you'll find additional ways to attract more money into your life?

The most important lesson that you'll learn from this account arises from the fact that you will never spend the principal, only the interest. This sends an extremely powerful message to your subconscious mind, a message that is even more important than having fun with money. It lets you know that you don't *need* money. By taking just a portion of what you earn and never using the principal (the amount you deposited), you're sending a message of abundance. There's money in this account that you will never need to use. What a powerful message! You'll never be broke again. You will *always* have money and you won't need all of it. After all, this is just money that you've spent over the years anyway and haven't been accounting for, so what's a few dollars accumulating in this account?

The financial independence account will produce profound changes in your subconscious as these two thoughts are instilled through active participation in this game:

• I will always have money, and
• I don't need money.

If you're like most people, these two new thoughts are just that, new. That's why the exercise of spending the interest as if you were already financially independent becomes as important as the habit of saving the money.

Remember Tim in chapter one, the gentleman I described as having earned and lived like a millionaire but who was hundreds of thousands of dollars in debt with no savings? You can assuredly avoid becoming like Tim if you pursue the strategy of this account. I'm sure you didn't identify him as being prosperous, possibly not even wealthy in your terms, but you'll always have money that you don't need and it will support your financial independence over time.

Bank Account #3:
My Purchases Account

The *purchases account* is the exact opposite of the financial independence account in that you *must* spend all of the money (interest and deposits) on a regular predetermined basis. You may choose to wait until it has accumulated to a certain amount or spend it at a scheduled and predetermined time, the first of every month for example, which I would recommend.

How often do you feel guilty about spending money? How often have you bought yourself some *guilty pleasure* (there's that language pattern again) and thought, "I can't really afford this and shouldn't be spending my money on this." But you do so anyway and then end up with a feeling of guilt that promotes a poverty consciousness that says, "There's not enough." This account will instill a new way of spending money, free of guilt, and will promote a new air of prosperity and abundance.

Since this account must be spent in its entirety, the money has already been pre-allocated for your spending pleasure. Have you ever set up an account that would allow you to buy whatever your heart desires without guilt and remorse? If we're doing it already, why not spend our money intelligently and in a methodical fashion that leaves us feeling more powerful at the end of the day?

The rule for the purchases account is the money must be spent on fun and whimsy; remember, we're playing a game here that will instill new healthy attitudes about money if you follow the rules.

Perhaps you've decided that the first Saturday of every

other month will be your allotted day to spend your purchases account, and this month you have amassed a total of
$28.04 for a spending spree. Find a location in your city that
is filled with fun shops and unique stores. If possible, try to
venture to a part of the city where you wouldn't normally
go and have no predetermined notion as to what you're
going to purchase with these funds.

Do you remember your piggy bank when you were a
child, and when you knew that it was full and you just had
to spend it? You didn't know what you were going to
spend it on—gum balls, new cars for your racetrack, or
those Barbie boots—but you knew you were going to
spend that money. Engage your inner child in this exercise
as much as "adultly" possible. Do not take the cash with
you on this journey, just the thought of your $28.04. Stroll
around this new section of your city and engage the merchants and peruse their wares. When something catches
your eye, not necessarily anything practical but something
that you might like to have, find out the cost. Ask the store
clerk to hold it for you for three days.

On your way home, fix your mind upon the item and
its price and plan to return three days later. The idea of this
time lag is to see if your subconscious will come up with
some creative way of attracting the $28.04 into your life,
even though you already have this amount in your
account. Perhaps someone who owes you money will suddenly pay you back or you might receive an unexpected
cheque in the mail, a refund or overpayment that's just
being returned now. These are both quite possible scenarios that would be welcome now that you are focused on
this amount of money.

A couple of words of caution: first, the manifestation of
this amount might not happen the very first time you play
the game. It might not happen for six months or longer, but
sooner or later magical occurrences of money popping into
your life, right at the time you're focusing on your purchases, will happen.

Second, be aware of multiples. You might not find the exact amount coming into your life right at the time you're playing this game but a day after you've played it you might receive a monthly raise at your job in the amount of $112.16, which is a multiple of four times the amount you were focusing on. The idea is first and foremost to create an awareness of attracting money into your life, to generate further abundance as you already have enough money for the item, and to have some fun with your old thoughts as you retrain your subconscious to believe that spending is guilt-free and joyful.

Each chapter in this book is based on discussions that arose during the course of my Girls Just Want to Have Funds group. This was as much of a learning experience for me as it was for the women in the group. The dialogue we shared and the ideas we discussed were illuminating to everyone.

At one of the meetings, I had presented the idea of the bank accounts. At the following meeting, the purchases account occupied centre stage in our discussions. I found that nearly half the group loved this particular account while the others experienced difficulty with the idea of spending all the money on themselves or on a frivolous purchase.

The half who loved this account (myself included) were the proclaimed spenders—we love to spend and have often felt guilty about our spending as we might have taken money from "pots" that should have been used for other purchases. All of the "easy spenders" thought this exercise would be a piece of cake, and it was, but something unusual occurred for most of this group. We all loved the idea that this money was earmarked for spending and all reported that it brought joy and fun back to our spending and eliminated the need for guilt as it was already designated spending. But the side benefit that most of us reported was that suddenly, again, myself included, we started to spend less and almost wanted to hold onto and hoard the funds in this account to some degree. As soon as we were supposed to spend the money, we encountered a slight resistance. It was not for the lack of funds but because this account felt so good and the spending was such a shift from guilt to enjoyment. Our portion of the group wanted to savour the experience.

What about the other half of the group—those women who reported they had great difficulty spending the money on themselves or on something that wasn't essential for them, their home, or their family? They reported that even though the money was earmarked for spending, they rarely spent money on themselves and felt guilty either way.

We took these women through the following process so they would remember the worth of their spending and that each dollar they spent on themselves would strengthen the economy and increase the income of their neighbours. Let's pretend that they found an item at a downtown strip mall but felt the money could be better used by giving it to charity or to their children. They felt that purchasing this trinket, to which their childlike mind was attracted, was just a waste of money.

If you belong to the second half of the group that I'm describing, try this conscious exercise: Think about the store owner from whom you're purchasing the item and the wholesaler who supplied it—think of how they are benefiting and staying open as a result of your purchase and how they are also able to serve the community and feed their children. What about the rental fee they pay their landlord and the taxes they pay to the city for the roads and the other municipal services they support as a result of your purchase? What about the snow removal services that stay in business by clearing this company's snow and the advertising firms that flourish as a result of the store owner's success and therefore their own? Keep going with this chain of thought until you really feel that your spending money on this relatively insignificant item will truly benefit both you and the economy.

What happens to the economy in a recession? People start to feel fearful and stop spending. Reduced spending hurts businesses, jobs are cut, and everyone feels the pain. The opposite is true when our economy is doing well—people spend, companies hire more workers to support the spending of the public, and everyone feels prosperous. Each time you spend, you're working at creating prosperity for your fellow citizens as well as for yourself. Remember this with each dollar you spend.

One last thought about this account. It might be convenient for you to take the time to return for your item several days later and you might find, for a number of reasons, you need to make your purchase on the spot. If this happens, you won't get the chance to give your mind the full opportunity for manifestation but you will still reap the benefits of the other positive spending habits. You might try focusing on your account and the amount that you will spend a few days beforehand. This could work just as well as the three-day holding period as you might attract the money before you even spend your account. Try it and see what happens for you!

Every dollar you deposit into this account and into the financial independence account will help you to form and reinforce positive habits around accumulating (saving) and spending money. You'll never need to worry about becoming like Bob. Remember Bob? He had millions of dollars in the bank, no family to share it with or leave his legacy to, and yet, in his eighties, he still lived as though the Depression was right around the corner. You'll never need to worry about spending or saving because you'll be reinforcing these new beliefs each time you make your deposits into these accounts. You'll get back in tune with that child who yearns to have fun with money again and the happiness that money can buy.

> Pleasure is the object, duty and
> the goal of all rational creatures.
> –Voltaire

The Importance of Pleasure

The main purpose of the purchases account is to establish or re-establish the power of pleasure, using money as a conduit. While I know that there are countless pleasures which money can't replace, there are just as many pleasures that only money can facilitate.

I remember a story from Charles Faulkner in his audio program *NLP: The New Technology of Achievement*. Faulkner talks about buying ice cream and that the only reason for doing so is pure pleasure. One doesn't eat ice cream for nourishment. It's only reason for existence is to delight the taste buds of the consumer. So what happens when we buy cheap ice-cream? Have you ever committed such a travesty? Be honest. I know that I have on occasion. And with each bite of that inferior brand, you remind yourself that you're not worth the full indulgence. You'll sacrifice a truly wonderful experience to save a couple of dollars, if that.

What other pleasurable experiences can you think of? How about listening to great music or going to a top-notch play? How about journeying first class the next time you fly or pampering yourself for an entire day at a spa? Take a few moments to list at least twenty pleasurable experiences. If you're having trouble coming up with twenty, then you really need this exercise. Ideally, you should have hundreds of items that come to mind with little effort. If you need help, call a friend or two for ideas about what they find enjoyable, luxurious, self-indulgent, and satisfying.

1. _____
2. _____
3. _____
4. _____
5. _____
6. _____
7. _____
8. _____
9. _____
10. _____

11. _____
12. _____
13. _____
14. _____
15. _____
16. _____
17. _____
18. _____
19. _____
20. _____

Joy is never in our power and pleasure often is.
–C. S. Lewis

The Pleasure Factor

You've no doubt heard by now about the coffee or latte factor in which you take that $1 per day minimum that you would spend on a cup of coffee and invest it for your retirement. Let's face it, it's more likely $2 to $5 dollars per day. I'd like to expand on this notion and introduce you to a fun game in addition to your new five bank accounts called The Pleasure Factor. I'd like you to purchase a piggy bank for yourself (perhaps you even have one lying around the house). It must be a fun bank that brings back positive memories from your childhood. You could simply use a glass jar but we're trying to reconnect with that child that still lives inside us and used to love and freely receive money.

Each day, I would like you to deposit at least $1, or more if you'd like. You could just start with all of the extra change lying around in your purse, house, or wallet. Each month or two, I'd like you to empty the contents of this bank and engage in an activity of pure pleasure. It might be getting a manicure or pedicure, buying exotic chocolates for yourself, or a great bottle of wine. Just as with a child, this is money that won't be missed or needed for bills or other expenditures. It would have been spent on your daily cup of coffee and long forgotten anyway. Why not compound the daily depositing of these coins for purely guilt-free pleasures. Have fun and I'm sure you'll be surprised at how much amasses in your piggy bank at each interval.

The following is a list from the kind and creative minds of my dear friends. You'll find a more detailed list on my web site www.thewomansguidetomoney.com. For the sake of saving paper, I've only included the top ten for each category but you'll find hundreds of ideas on the web site. I can't take credit for most of these ideas. I put an S.O.S. e-mail out to my friends for their ideas and couldn't believe how many creative concepts they all came back with. I was surprised that all of my friends seemed to have the most ideas for the $20 and under category. Send out an e-mail to your friends for even more ideas and I'd love to hear from you too!

> An inordinate passion for pleasure
> is the secret of remaining young.
> –Oscar Wilde

Top Ten Under $20

If you save $1 per day, you can empty your piggy bank for something in this category just about every two weeks.

- Treat yourself to a gustatory pleasure: exotic chocolates or fruit, a package of special roast coffee beans, desserts, a bottle of wine.
- Make a long-distance phone call to a great friend that you haven't chatted with for some time.
- Visit a museum, art gallery, or go stargazing at your planetarium.
- Go for a picnic.
- Frame a special holiday or vacation picture.
- Buy matching napkins and/or napkin rings.
- Get yourself a special hand cream for the winter season.
- Buy a great self-tanner or a tanning package.

- Purchase a new CD of your favorite music.
- Buy yourself cut flowers.

Top Ten Under $30

At just $1 per day, you can indulge in this category every month.

- Treat yourself to dinner or a leisurely lunch. Better yet, take yourself to brunch at the best hotel in your city.
- Get a sexy new haircut.
- Buy a book or a cookbook and try a new recipe each month—find a few friends willing to do the same and have a pot luck every thirty days.
- Book a yoga or Tai Chi lesson or a session with a personal trainer.
- Buy some paint and repaint your bathroom.
- Purchase some sexy undies, pajamas, or other nightwear just for you.
- Book a massage.
- Have a spa night at home.
- Host a game night: buy a favourite old game (such as Monopoly) and have your friends over (have them bring the munchies).
- Buy some new bathroom and kitchen towels or an apron.

Top Ten Under $60

Luxury comes at just $1 per day every two months or bump it up to $2 per day and enjoy this category monthly. You deserve it!

- Indulge in a massage, facial, pedicure or manicure.
- Buy yourself and a friend cut flowers.
- Book a limo night for you and a few friends—the more friends, the longer the ride or the lesser the cost.
- Take a friend out for desserts and cocktails.

- Book a belly-dancing lesson.
- Have a sleepover with a friend and rent a movie; enjoy a bottle of wine and other treats (ice cream, antipasto, and decadent cheese and crackers).
- Go horseback riding.
- Pay to have your home cleaned.
- Go to an arcade or casino.
- Buy new shoes, a new purse, or a lovely sweater, scarf, or gloves.

> A large income is the best recipe
> for happiness I ever heard of.
> –Jane Austen

Bank Account #4:
My Annual Income Account

What if you could take a year off "just because"? What if you could save enough money to do this at regular intervals throughout your life and do it without the need for a paycheque? What if you could just take one month or a few months off to pursue your hobbies or other interests without any fear about how you're going to pay the bills? You've guessed it; the purpose of the *annual income account* is to regularly save a portion of your excess funds to support your next (and possibly first) sabbatical.

So many of my clients who are over sixty have sung a mantra of sorts during their entire working career and it goes like this: "One day, when I retire, I'll finally have the time to do [fill in the blank]." The unfortunate part of that goal is that they did not savour life because their focus was on an event far in the future. And, as statistics show, many people become severely ill or die a year into retirement. Why wouldn't you take hold of life as you go along instead of putting it on hold until "one day"?

How much money would you need in an account to support you for a month, six months, or a year? How would you feel about going to work each day knowing that your sabbatical is right around the corner? We're not talking about vacation time here, although it could be one of your goals with this account. This is a time when you would be free to pursue other interests aside from your work—write a book, visit your city's libraries and museums, read the newspaper until noon, spend more quality time with your children, or just experience a period of leisure. What's the amount that you would need in an account for this notion to become a reality without the worry of earning a living? It's likely less than you think. Would you still need to drive during this time? Perhaps during your sabbatical you could park your car, and thereby reduce the insurance cost and save hundreds of dollars per month on gas.

Heck, you're not rushing off to work and appointments during this time, so you might find that you don't need a car at all during your sabbatical. You might take three months off in the summer and choose to walk to your various destinations and take an occasional cab ride home from the grocery store. Not only might you enjoy the feeling of being a tourist, as you walk instead of driving, but you might find that eliminating certain payments could make this account achieve its purpose sooner. Fix an amount in your mind for this account and work towards getting there. Notice the newfound joy you experience with each deposit to this account as you dream about what you'll do during your next, or first, sabbatical.

Bank Account #5:
My Investment Account

In the *investment account*, you will focus your energy and money on investments and learn to enjoy your investments for greater profit and ease. If you're already putting a predetermined monthly amount into an RRSP account, you might wish to skip this account or create an entirely new one. Superficially, this account might seem similar to the financial independence account; where it differs is the active investment participation and experience that I want you to derive from it. Remember, with the financial independence account, all amounts you deposit must go into a safe interest-bearing account. This leaves little room for you to practice your investment savvy.

As the investment account makes a profit at predetermined levels, I would encourage you to take the excess profit and redistribute it as you would any other income. For example, if you have just made a profit of $1,500 from the sale of a successful stock pick, distribute the profit by first placing it in the income account and then distributing it to your other accounts. As your investments rise in value and you actively move the profits around, you'll be training your subconscious that profits are fun and allow you to play more money games. Remember to do this with small amounts as well as large. A $10 profit is as important as a $1,000 profit or a half-million-dollar profit. If we don't teach our conscious and subconscious mind how to deal with the small profits well, how can we move up to dealing with the larger ones? Is it any wonder that certain lottery winners in Canada are actually worse off after a few years than they were before they won the money? They have had no incremental training in how to deal with money, especially that much money.

You might be thinking that many of your investments have not been profitable, especially given the recent volatility of most North American and world stock markets. Remember that investing takes all shapes and forms. When we refer to investing, it may be in the stock market; it could be the purchase of a piece of real estate on your own or with someone; or it could involve opening the business of your dreams. We're playing a game again with our subconscious, and want to instill the rules that lead to healthy investing attitudes every step of the way.

If you find yourself holding an investment that continues to lose money, or has lost money right from the start, you can choose to get rid of it sooner rather than later. Let's say, for example, you've just purchased XYZ stock for $1,000. The next day you see it decline to $910 and the day after that it's down still further to $880. You look at this investment and call your broker who suggests that it could just keep going down and you realize this investment is not profitable. "If all of my investments are profitable, then this investment must not be mine." But what if the opposite happens? What if it turns around quickly the next week and you miss out on something really good? Don't worry; there are enough opportunities in the market for you to make profits in various ways for years to come. Minimize your losses and ride the gains for maximum growth in order to make all of your investments more profitable.

A caveat applies if you have invested in a portfolio with a financial advisor or planner. Always check with your advisor before selling any investment portfolio that might have fallen temporarily because of overall market conditions and that might have fees or charges for deciding to liquidate. Read and digest the fine print *before* you make or sell an investment.

Attitudes Towards Money

People have always tended to have different goals for different pots of money. Some of my clients have been overly cautious about investing their RRSP portfolios even though they have twenty years or more until retirement and thus have the time to invest in higher-risk and potentially higher-yielding investments. And it still shocks me to this day that many of my clients will view their tax refund as "found money," even though the government is returning to them the excess taxes that they have paid throughout the year. They'll often blow this money on shopping sprees, a new fridge, a television, or something for the house that really isn't needed. The thinking seems to be that since this is money they didn't expect to receive, it can be spent spontaneously or imprudently.

Let's say you were in the market for a new sweater and decided to look for one at the local shopping mall. You find just the one you were hoping for and it's in your price range—$100. Just as you're getting ready to pay for the sweater, you spot a good friend in the store and she tells you that there's an identical sweater on sale at the other end of the mall for $50 less. Unable to pass up a 50% discount, you put down the sweater and trudge to the other end of the mall even though your feet are nearly killing you.

Now let's pretend that a week later you're in the market for a new stereo system. You and your partner have been saving up for a year and it's finally time to purchase the very best. Just as you've totalled up your purchases, after spending hours testing out the latest equipment and questioning the sales associate, your good friend strolls in again. She tells you that a sound system identical to the one that you're about to purchase for $2,550 can be found just a few miles away for only $2,500. Do you drop everything and go? Likely not, as the percentage of savings is small, just over 2%. So why wouldn't you hop in your car and drive a couple of miles to save the same $50 that you were willing to walk with your sore feet to save on the sweater? Why does it matter if the $50 savings represents 50% or 2%? It's still the same $50!

Not only do we do funny things when calculating savings, when it comes to spending money, we can also do strange things.

The story of the "Man in the Green Bathrobe" is told by Gary Belsky and Thomas Gilovich in their book *Why Smart People Make Big Money Mistakes and How To Correct Them* to illustrate the concept of mental accounting as defined by behavioral economists.

As legend has it, the man in the green bathrobe is on the last day of his honeymoon and before retiring for bed that evening, he sees something on his dresser stand. He notices that it's a $5 casino chip—the last of the couple's gambling allowance. He can't very well leave this chip behind and will not embarrass himself by cashing it in, so he decides to sneak downstairs in his green housecoat for one last bet.

He puts the chip down on a roulette table and on his lucky number, 17. Sure enough, the ball hits 17 and pays a 35-1 bet, which yields him nearly $200. He lets his winnings stand and his luck continues as the ball lands on 17 and his winnings grow to over $6,000. And so it goes on until the lucky groom is about to place a bet for several million dollars. At that point the pit boss intervenes and tells the man that the casino doesn't have enough funds to accept the bet. The man decides to move down the Vegas strip to the best hotel in the city. He again places his entire bet upon the lucky 17 and his luck holds, yielding him this time hundreds of millions of dollars. Feeling that his lucky streak will never end, he bets it all once again. However, this time the ball lands on 18 and he loses everything. He leaves broke and devastated and even has to walk several miles back to his hotel.

When he finally gets back to his room, his wife asks him where he's been.

"I was playing roulette," he says softly.

"Well, how did you do?"

"Oh, not bad, I only lost five dollars."

The moral of this story is that at any point, starting with the $5 chip, which then grew into millions and millions of dollars, the money was always his. But because he only considered the $5 to be his and the rest of the winnings to belong to the casino, he felt he could take more chances than he might otherwise have done. Do you suppose this fellow would have cashed out his retirement savings to play the tables in Vegas or, if he had, would have made silly bets such as risking the entire pot with each and every wager? Probably not. Although you may or may not be able to relate to this gambling story, what about other pots of money you've identified as not really being yours? Is that how you see the income tax refund, which is your money being returned to you, and without interest I might add, or the inheritance from the death of a loved one, which some consider "blood money"?

By using the Five Bank Account system for all the money you receive from all sources, you can effectively ignore the origin of the different pots of money (i.e. salary, bonuses, winnings, inheritances) and focus more on which pots of money the funds will go into. So instead of blowing a bonus from work, your focus will turn towards the purpose of your new account system. Whether it's spending the balance of the purchases account regularly or putting a portion of your bonus into the financial independence account, your focus will be on a new purpose for your money, and not on its source.

Your Five Bank Accounts Recap

Choose the Right Type of Bank

In Canada, we have one of the best Internet banking systems in the world. You can pay almost every bill imaginable online, have your paycheque deposited directly into your account, and transfer funds at the click of a button.

Take a look at what your bank has to offer before you play the account system game and shop around for one that will accommodate your needs. Do you need to have the accounts at separate banks to ensure that you follow the instructions and aren't tempted to spend the money? If so, you'll also have to make trips each month to those banks in order to make the deposits, so keep that in mind when choosing a bank.

Personally, I enjoy the convenience of using one bank and was shocked, but pleasantly surprised, to find out that, as an existing customer, I can open as many new accounts as I want with just a few clicks of my mouse. And much to my delight, and that of the little child inside me, my Internet banking service even allows customers to name their accounts. Each time I log in, I'm reinforcing the game and the positive money habits I've developed. You can even choose to hide certain account balances when you log on, so you won't be tempted to use those amounts in calculations for bill payments and other spending. Shop around and find the right banking system for your game.

How Long Should You Play?

That's entirely up to you. I personally intend to play this game for the rest of my life. It's fun and it's like going to the gym to maintain a healthy body. I keep these accounts running just to ensure that my focus on money remains healthy.

Creating Other Accounts

After I realized how easy it was with Internet banking to open additional accounts, I quickly opened a couple more. I loved the idea of a tithing account and also added an education account as both have significant meaning in my life. You could open a lovers' account, where you save money for you and your spouse—it could be spent on romantic dinners throughout the year, a New Year's cruise, or whatever else would allow you to explore your romantic side. This way, when you need more romance in your life, the money will be there to cover the cost of creating the mood you desire, while adding more pleasure to your experience with money.

Whatever the account, just ensure that you set the rules at the start and that the spending of either the funds in the account or the interest takes place at regular predetermined intervals. Have fun. There are no limits, and you can change the percentages to suit your life.

Sharing Your Experience

One of the most effective ways to fix in the mind any new concept is to teach it! Gather a group of your girlfriends and explain to them the Five Bank Account system. As you do, you will further instill the teachings into your subconscious and conscious mind. And as you play and share your experiences, you'll gain valuable insights into how your friends are playing the game. What new accounts do they set up? What experiences are they reporting? Not only will you benefit from the support of your friends but you'll also be helping them create valuable and positive money habits while you enjoy their company.

Visit www.thewomansguidetomoney.com for a full information kit that includes guidelines and rules for setting up your own money group for prosperity in your life now!

Summary

- Embrace the child inside you who used to have fun with money. Stop saving for emergencies and start playing for a positive financial future.
- You can easily live on 90% of what you earn for the rest of your life. A part of all that you earn is yours to keep.
- Set up the Five Bank Account system today. Change or add accounts as you like, but always keep the first three accounts for maximum wealth and enjoyment.
- Be confident in the affirmations that you now don't need money and you will always have money as a result of playing the bank account games.

Your Prosperity Action Steps

- Open your bank accounts today. At least open three dedicated accounts or determine if you already can use some of your current accounts and rename them. Determine how many accounts you would like to have and ensure that you play with the first three as a minimum. Decide what other accounts you'd like to open such as a lovers' account or an education account. Determine how long you would like to play for and what bank(s) will best suit your needs. Finally, either label your passbook or rename your accounts online if you have access to Internet banking; make this game appealing to the child within you.

- Share your experiences with others. During the next week, teach at least one person the Five Bank Account system. By teaching the system to others, you will reinforce the ideas in your own mind and you will likely learn valuable insights from those you teach it to as well.

- List at least fifty actions or activities that you will engage in when you're financially independent. If the ideas flow, keep going. If you need a little support, just visit my web site at www.thewomans-guidetomoney.com for more ideas. Remember, what you focus on expands. This is an important step and you deserve to be wealthy!

- Obtain your piggy bank this week. Find a fun bank that conjures excitement and playfulness regarding money. Remember to deposit at least $1 per day in your "bank" and be aware of the money that you find everywhere—in your car, on the sidewalk, between your sofa cushions. Deposit everything you find in your new "bank," remember to empty it periodically, and drop me a line too to let me know about your purchases at www.thewomans-guidetomoney.com.

Chapter Five
The Plan

Congratulations! I'm so proud that you've made it to the second half of *The Woman's Guide to Money*. The latter half of your journey through this book will explore self-esteem and self-image issues, goal setting, handling and overcoming your fears, and finding your ideal career path.

After reading chapter one and our discussion about *you* as your most important investment, it is my wish that you truly understand this to the core of your being; it is essential for your advancement on your journey to greater wealth, success, happiness, abundance, and peace.

Eight Steps to Achieving Your Goals

We all have the same 24 hours in a day—it's one of the few things in life that *is* equal for us all. So how are you spending your 24 hours?

Successful people have just as many challenges and problems as everyone else, they've just learned to solve them better. You're never going to forever rid yourself of problems. What's your definition of success? Are you setting yourself up for success or for failure?

How Do You Define Success?

What does it matter if you were successful last year if you are not now on the road to a new and worthier goal this year? Each night when you go to bed and each morning when you awake, you have only yourself to answer to. Are you defining success on your own terms or according to the terms of your peer group, friends, family, or colleagues?

What do you personally define as success? Do financial achievements, emotional and spiritual growth, friends, and hobbies form part of your definition of success? As you consider what success means to you, ponder the words of Ralph Waldo Emerson and his wisdom from over a century past:

To laugh often and much;
To win the respect of intelligent people and the affection of children;
To earn the appreciation of honest critics and endure the betrayal of false friends;
To appreciate beauty, to find the best in others;
To leave the world a bit better, whether by a healthy child, a garden patch, or a redeemed social condition;
To know even one life has breathed easier because you have lived.
This is to have succeeded.

> Many of life's failures are people
> who did not realize how close they
> were to success when they gave up.
> –Thomas Edison

Life's a Cookie

Life and our universe are magically and wonderfully mathematical in nature. If you suffer from innumeracy, not to worry. It's really as simple as a cookie recipe.

Let's assume for a moment that we'd like to make a batch of traditional chocolate chip cookies. There are certain ingredients that we must have on hand. We know we need sugar, butter, chocolate chips, and flour. The other ingredients are important too, but the four ingredients I just mentioned are the basics of our recipe. If we take the flour, for example, and want to make our cookies a bit healthier than the norm, we can exchange the less nutritious white flour and substitute whole wheat, rice, or even kamut flour. However, we do need some type of binding agent. Should we stray too far from the norm and mistake the ingredient of flour for apple sauce, we will likely end up with a mess for the garbage—it certainly wouldn't result in chocolate chip cookies.

Life As a Recipe

Life isn't much different. There's always a methodical and logical recipe for anything we'd like to achieve in life. Sure, we can personalize the recipe and deviate from the norm with secret ingredients but, just as with math, 5+6+4 will always equal 15. Change the sequence of the numbers, move them around or even break the 6 down to two 3s, you'll still end up with 15. This is the way of our universe. So why are we perplexed when we change the numbers around and don't end up with the correct number or result?

Many years ago, I listened to a conversation a friend of mine was having with my mom. She was complaining about her weight and that she just couldn't shed any of her excess pounds, which were many. Her ten-year-old son piped up with the magic solution (it was so easy for him). He said, "Mom, if you want to lose weight, just eat less and exercise more." Simple, right? Eat less and/or more health-fully and exercise more or more efficiently. Yet why do so many North Americans remain obese and overweight? It's actually become an epidemic in our country. While other countries are dying from malnutrition and a lack of the basics, we're dying from the lack of understanding of a simple formula that would stop many of the diseases caused by inactivity and obesity.

Regardless of your definition of success or the end result you're looking for, there's a logical mathematical for-mula that when followed will produce success for you. The important elements within the formula will ensure that you are on the path to achievement, but, more important, it will also ensure that the journey is enjoyed along the way.

I've created a simple formula that even those who are fearful of math can follow. In chapter one we briefly looked back at our childhood and where certain core thoughts and beliefs about wealth, money, and prosperity originated. We could spend an eternity trying to figure out exactly when and where our lax thoughts or inability to manifest or retain wealth came from. We could blame our parents and what we came into this world with and find the same problems popping up until the day we die, or we can consciously change our life in an elegant, methodical, and more empowering fashion with my simple success formula.

Your Daily Success Formula:
Appreciation + Focus + Strategies + Action = Success

Most financial books simply focus on strategies, which are definitely important. They're the flour of our cookie recipe. But if we don't enjoy the process along the way, we'll end up like Bob, or worse, we'll have the same fate as the lottery winner or Tim.

Appreciation

One need look no further than the life of a quickly famous movie star. Why do so many turn to drugs and alcohol when they have it all? Money, fame, friends, all that one desires, yet all too often we read about these stars turning to deadly substances to find "more" or that something that's missing.

Appreciating everything that shows up in your life and being grateful for what doesn't or hasn't shown up yet is essential. Do you know someone who is lucky? If you model and interview the "lucky" person, they almost always tend to be extremely grateful for what they have in life even when they don't have much. The result? They usually attract more of it into their life.

Use your elastic band exercise to practice daily appreciation for all that you have in your life and make it a lifelong habit.

Focus

Our second ingredient requires us to become experts at being deletion creatures. Once we've set our goals, and you will by the end of this chapter, focusing on what we want is critical. We must keep our attention clear on our desired goal and avoid all that puts our attention on what we don't want.

Turn off the news. Change the subject with those around you who always talk about all that is wrong with the world even though they're not willing to do anything to change it. Fill your mind and life with events, activities, people and stimulus that assists you on your mission in life.

> An investment in knowledge
> always pays the best interest.
> –Benjamin Franklin

Strategies

Although I chose not to focus on the hardline financial strategies that will help you build wealth and invest your money more efficiently, they are still an important element of the success equation. Pick up a couple of financial books from your library and learn about your money, credit, our banking system, and so much more. If you have access to the Internet, a world of information is at your fingertips. Learn one new financial definition per week as a start, then move towards implementing necessary financial strategies in your own life. Start with an affirmation such as, "I'm now joyfully earning more than I spend," or, "I'm now joyfully spending less than I earn."

I don't know your definition of success but I know that using the success equation will exponentially propel you towards your goal and with greater ease, happiness, and enjoyment.

Step One:

Why Haven't You Set Your Goals?

> I am not discouraged because every wrong
> attempt discarded is another step forward.
> –Thomas Edison

Fear is, in my opinion, the number one reason why we don't set specific goals, whether large or small, in our lives. We can think of a million reasons for not setting goals— we're too busy, we'll do it tomorrow, we'll wait until New Year's and make it a resolution, and on and on. People who write out specific goals, even if they then hide the list away in a drawer and never look at it again, are more likely to achieve those goals than those who don't write them out. So if it's that simple, why don't we do it? If all we had to do was determine what we wanted and write it down to be more likely to achieve it, wouldn't it make sense to just do it?

> A shy failure is nobler
> than an immodest success.
> –Kahlil Gibran

Setting a "goal" can be a daunting task that starts to force your conscious mind to examine where you are and where you'd like to go. Our fear of moving forward can often stop us from even daydreaming about how things could be better. After all, life's not that bad, right? You're doing okay, and if you rock the boat, your life might get worse. Your job isn't all that bad, even though you start to get those butterflies around 6 p.m. Sunday night when you realize that Monday morning is just a few short hours away.

But what if it could be better? I love Deepak Chopra's explanation of why we settle for a life that's less than it could be. In *A Path to Love*, he sums it up by saying that we choose a life of "known hells" over "unknown heavens." It's much easier for most of us to live in a self-imposed "hell" because of its familiarity. "Heaven" is possible but it's unknown and scary so we don't even dare dream of the possibilities that are available to us. We pity ourselves, view those who achieve their dreams as "lucky," and go about our daily routines.

> Now and then I go about pitying myself
> and all the while my soul is being
> blown by great winds across the sky.
> –Ojibwa saying

There is greatness within you that needs only to be directed for you to achieve a life that is greater than you could ever imagine. You were born an original and there is a great purpose for you, and only *for you.* Comfort is your greatest enemy.

As Einstein believed, doing the same thing over and over again is the recipe for insanity. I would add that complaining about your life situation but not doing anything to alter it would further add to a life of frustration and insanity. For our own edification and to keep our self-esteem healthy, complaints without action can be debilitating. I highly recommended that if you'd prefer to not make a change in your life, at least be fair and reserve complaint. If you're overweight and constantly tired, for example, but still haven't committed to a workout regime or a healthier diet, resist the urge to mentally or verbally express complaint.

Haven't we all been there in our lives? Perhaps you're there right now. You moan and complain about your relationship, your job, your friends, and your family, but you do nothing about it. You just moan and groan when you could just as easily get up and do something about your life.

Step Two:
It All Starts with the 24 Hours You Have

> The time is always right
> to do what is right.
> –Martin Luther King

"If only" and "one day" are the twin enemies that you will encounter on your path to what you desire. "If only" I had more time, more intellect, more money, more you-name-it, but the most popular excuse by far is the lack of time. One of the only things that is equal for all in life, and something that we have in common even with the billionaires and those whom we view as successful, is the fact that we share the same 24 hours in a day. No more, no less. It's what you do with these 24 hours that makes the difference. And what about our lamentable "one day"? Today is the only day you really have. There is no guarantee that we're going to be here tomorrow. "One day" must become "today," so why not do what you can now? The only thing I can assure you of is that if you're counting on "one day," that day has arrived and it's called today!

> Always the more beautiful answer
> who asks the more beautiful question.
> –e. e. cummings

Now, what if you set out to discover your goal and actually achieve it? If you could realize what is now a dream, how would your life change? Sounds simple and crazy, doesn't it? Remember our negative exercise in chapter two about visualizing a major disease? If you're like most people to whom I've told about this exercise, every fibre in your being recoiled at the thought. If it is so easy to believe that visualizing a major disease will cause it to develop, couldn't it be that simple to achieve your goals?

Most people tell me that the most difficult part of writing down their goals is their own lack of clarity about what they actually want. Some don't like their jobs but might not know what else they'd like to do. Here are two exercises to get you jump-started.

The first, offered by Jack Canfield and Mark Victor Hansen in *The Aladdin Factor,* consists of the "perfect day" exercise, which can help even the most uncreative person determine a wants list.

> Life isn't about finding yourself.
> Life is about creating yourself.
> –George Bernard Shaw

Find a quiet place in your home and allow at least 15 to 30 minutes of relaxed but focused daydreaming. Envision what an ideal day might look, sound, and feel like to you. The subconscious cannot distinguish between that which is vividly imagined and that which is real. Make this experience as rich and detailed as possible, and when you're finished, take the time to write down all that you desire, or, keep a tape recorder close by and record your thoughts verbally as you envision your perfect day.

You might wish to do this exercise again after you've finished this chapter and focus on all of the values that you will list in step five that follows. It's essential that your mind has a picture of what an ideal day in your life could be in the future so that it has a picture to direct it.

If your goal was to take a trip to Maui, although financially it might be a decade away until you can afford such a journey, the idea of locating a travel brochure and possibly posting pictures of your dream vacations could get you there sooner. Our life is made up of moments and then days. By knowing what a perfect day might feel and look like, we have a greater chance of achieving it.

As you relax and daydream, run your mind through a full 24-hour period. Who might you wake up with and where? What does your home, bedroom, and bathroom look like? Are there children or grandchildren nearby? Will you rush off to a CEO position or have the freedom to relax and read the paper with a flexible career? What will you do during the day? Will you have a health break, a walk, or run at lunch? What will you do when the day is done? What car or transportation will bring you home? The more detail you can produce, the better. Have fun and remember that this is your ideal day and your sacred journey in creating the road map to your life.

Being aware of what you truly desire is the first and most important step. You'll be amazed at the magic or coincidences that start to happen in your life once you've focused on those desires. Suddenly, people who can help you achieve your goals will just show up or books on your bookshelf will grab your attention and provide the answer you are looking for. Once you've commanded your subconscious to go after something, watch it happen. It's been said that when the student is ready, the teacher will appear. The teacher might have been there all along but until you, the student, were ready, you couldn't see the teachings offered. Look closely at your life for the teachers and teachings right under your nose.

Another very simple exercise that might help you identify what you want, even before you spell out an actual goal, asks you to look at the people you envy. Look at what they have, what their life is like, and what it is about them that you envy. As you do this, remember to bless them for what they have—that which you don't currently have but would like. If you were to curse them for what they have, it would remind you of what you don't have and instill in yourself the belief that what they have is wrong. This will only prevent it from manifesting in your own life. If, for example, you're envious of your best friend's new 10,000-square-foot house, wouldn't it make more sense for you to value your friend's achievement and learn how she did it so that one day you could own such a home? How can you expect to manifest it in your own life if it's wrong for your friend to have this home? Either you'll never achieve a home like your friend's because you've already identified your friend's achievement as wrong or you'll be unhappy with yourself if you do get a home like that because you have already instilled negative thoughts about such an achievement.

Step Three:
Are Your Goals Realistic?

Are you setting yourself up for failure? I have a wonderful friend who recently shared with me his goal of having his company do well enough to pay him a salary of $600,000 per year. Since I've known him, his company has rarely been able to pay him more than $50,000 per year. When I inquired further as to how he planned to reach this corporate goal, his answers were vague and not well thought out. When I asked him how he would rate himself based on his corporate goals, he told me that year in and year out, he feels like a failure. Is it possible that's he's setting himself up to fail?

My friend never took the time to analyze his goals on a rudimentary cause-and-effect scale. He never even thought through all of the planning and other details that go into moving from an annual salary of $50,000 a year to $600,000 a year. If he had cognitively and realistically thought out his goal, he would have realized that he's not willing to go through the sacrifices and hours of work and dedication that would be needed to move his salary to over half a million per year. So why have such a lofty goal and continue to feel like a failure? Why not create goals that will incrementally move you towards their achievement and the well-being that comes with being a success?

Let's subject our goals to an acid test of sorts. Is there an alignment between our higher goals and our values and, most important, are we willing to do what it would take to achieve these goals? If we're not, then why set them and ourselves up for failure?

Step Four:
Discovering Your Values

Once you've laid the foundation for discovering your true values in life, it's easy to set clear and obtainable goals. The process of setting your goals will help clarify the worthiness of those goals.

It is unrealistic to expect that the goals you had in your early twenties, whether written down or not, will stay the same in your thirties, forties, and after retirement. Every mother will attest that once she's had her first child, everything in her life changed, including her values, so why would and any of us expect our goals to remain constant?

What's important to you? What do you live for when you wake up each morning? Values and feelings are likely to be attached to the goals that you've identified for yourself. If you'd like to earn more money at work, it's not the money you're after but the freedom and security that the increased money will bring. What will freedom and security add to your life? It may afford you the luxury of a first-class education for your child or give you more time to spend with friends and loved ones. A goal of an increased wage at work or a better-paying job doesn't create an inspiring mental image in and of itself. You must identify the value and feeling that lie at the core of the goal.

> I would never die for my beliefs
> because I might be wrong.
> –Betrand Russell

You can identify all of the ways you can be successful in your life in addition to the main goal. Suppose you want a better relationship with your spouse. This is your goal. The values and feelings you desire might be passion, love, and excitement. A better relationship is a by-product and is only one way that you can feel these things in your life.

Take a moment to list all of the values that are important to you. I'll get you started with a number of universal values:

- Freedom
- Security
- Family
- Love
- Passion
- Growth
- Satisfaction
- Happiness
- Independence
- Fun
- Success
- Spirituality
- Integrity
- Creativity
- Power
- Challenge
- Respect
- _____
- _____
- _____
- _____
- _____
- _____
- _____
- _____

One way to start is by selecting the most important categories and then listing the specific values from each group. For example, your *family values* might include love, freedom, and security, while your *career values* might be quite different and include growth, creativity, and challenge. I encourage you to look at the grouping below and consider these categories in terms of your life and the specific values that are important to you in each category.

- Family
- Career
- Relationships/friends
- Health and vitality
- Religion/spirituality
- Hobbies
- Personal growth
- Community involvement
- _____
- _____
- _____
- _____

Now take a moment to identify all the ways that you can experience these values in your life and some specific goals and changes that you need to introduce into your life to intensify them.

- _____
- _____
- _____
- _____
- _____

In step five, we'll identify a simple model for testing your goals against the values that you've identified as important to you. You might determine that some of these aren't right for you.

Step Five:
The Acid Test

There is a great law in our universe that can and should be applied to many areas of your life and, when understood, will create a clarity in life that will make goal setting easy and effortless. This great law is *the law of cause and effect*. This law simply states that the effect must, and always will, follow a cause.

For example, if you were to sit in front of a fire and throw in a little kindling and paper, you'll likely have just a small fire. Throw a few logs on, and the heat will surely come. But, as we know with a fire, it's also the care and attention that we pay to it that keeps it burning and warming our home for hours. To simply start the fire and walk away will produce only temporary heat. How often have you sat in front of your metaphorical fire and said to it, "Give me some heat and I'll give you wood?" So if we wish our fire to burn all night long, we must tend to it and take those actions that are necessary for a night of heat. The *effects* we experience in life can always be traced back to the *causes* we have focused on engaging.

Although it might seem that I'm stating the obvious, it's shocking to me how often people, including myself, forget this simple universal law and focus entirely on the effect, forgetting that the causes are what will eventually produce it. Think of this principle in terms of a grand apothecary scale—causes on the left side and effects on the right. Filling the left side and focusing our efforts there will always, with time, lift the scale to an equal or greater degree.

As you develop your life goals, try this simple acid test for determining if your goals are worthy of you. Take a blank sheet of paper and draw a line down the middle of it. On the right-hand side, write your goal (the effect) and note a few reasons for obtaining this goal and why achieving it is important to you. On the left-hand side, think creatively and list all of the actions you'll have to take to reach this goal (the causes). Once you've completed this exercise, look back at your values list in step four and determine whether the causes and the required action steps align with the values that you've identified.

I'll take you through a simple example that I personally tried. It created great clarity for the setting of my own goals, but the exercise also identified a values conflict that I might otherwise never have discovered or discovered much later.

When I completed this exercise a number of years ago, my top two life values were family and career. Within my family values, I identified love, freedom, and respect as my top priorities (we'll identify specifics in step eight). Within my career values, my list named growth, challenge, and money.

I then pulled out my blank sheet of paper, put "career goals" at the top and listed on the right all the goals that aligned with my career values. At the time, I was also contemplating opening my own business with the aim of achieving greater financial growth than I knew would be possible with my employment at the time.

The left side of my sheet of paper listed all of the tasks and action steps that would be necessary to achieve my goals. Before completing this exercise, I knew that my three career values were growth, challenge, and money but I didn't know their order of importance until I saw them written down on paper. When it came to determining the specific financial reward that would satisfy my goal of wealth, I decided on the lofty amount of a half-million-dollar salary within three years. The mistake I had made in pulling a number out of the air was evident within a few minutes. I quickly realized that very long hours of work, continual education, and all that it would take to move me to such a high salary in a short time was more than I was willing to do.

It wasn't until I had finished my list of "family values" and identified the goals that aligned with my values of love, freedom, and respect that I recognized some major conflicts. When I wrote down my family values on paper, freedom quickly became my top priority—freedom to spend more time with the ones I love. When I glanced at my "career list," I knew there was a problem. How could I find more time to achieve balance in my life when I was creating goals that were simply going to steal too much of my time?

Discovering and understanding what's important to you leads to life decisions that are easier to make. A single mother, for example, might determine that "security" and "freedom" are the most important family values. Security could mean a steady paycheque and freedom the ability to have more time to spend with the children and friends. Why then should one minute be spent entertaining the notion of starting a new business? I'm not saying by any means that a single mother couldn't do this; many have, and very successfully. Can you see how a woman whose priorities are security and the freedom to have lots of free time might be setting herself up for failure by opening a new company entailing great risk and many overtime hours?

Save these sheets of paper and treat them as the scrapbook of your life. Review them often as a living document and revise them when necessary. Your goals and values will change over time and, by understanding that they have, you will achieve a greater balance and will be able to re-adjust the order of your priorities. Whether you write your goals and values down or not, think back just ten short years to see how your values have changed. I have not been blessed with children yet, but my career and all other goals and values would change should I suddenly learn that I had a little one on the way.

Think back to the example of the single mother. Wouldn't it make more sense for her to plan on opening the business after the children are in school or even after they've left the house entirely? At that time, security might no longer rank as a primary goal because she doesn't have to provide for her children. In its place, passion or challenge could move into the top positions. I often think of the basic idea that we can do anything but we can't do everything. When it comes to our personal goals, why not set up the rules so we can win?

Many wonderful books have been written on goal setting and aligning your values with those goals. This chapter only makes a small dent when it comes to setting your life goals, but I encourage you to start and, in times of emotional conflict, write down your goals and values or priorities. Compare them regularly and you'll likely discover, as I did, that you might be setting yourself up for failure before you've even started.

Step Six:
Creating A Higher Purpose

Of all of the goals, values, and wants in life (and there are many), you must have a higher vision or purpose for your life that you can ultimately compare against all else. A statement of world renowned psychologist Abraham Maslow is one that I quickly knew I would adopt forever. In his book *Motivation and Personality*, Maslow states that people who know themselves well, should "be independent of the good opinion of other people." I wrote this quote down, later typed it and printed it out, and stuck it on my fridge for months. I truly strive to be "independent of the good opinion of other people" and often fail miserably. But each time I set a new goal or write down a desire, I compare it against my higher vision of myself. For example, if I were to strive for a new car or suit, I would list all of the extra hours I would need to work to pay for it, and I would ask myself if it is truly for me or just to impress my friends and others.

Do you have a higher vision for your life—one that you can compare against all others and that brings clarity and meaning to your life? Perhaps it's one of love or care for our earth. If you haven't found your higher vision yet, allow yourself to be open to this notion and choose a purpose that is larger than life. If it's not perfect, change it over time, but decide on a vision and make each moment of your life a step towards this ideal you.

> The only man who is really free is the one
> who can turn down an invitation
> to dinner with out giving an excuse.
> –Jules Renard

Step Seven:
Chunking

Think about the old saying, "How do you eat an elephant?" And of course the answer is, "One bite at a time." Rome might not have been built in a day, but each day brings a fresh and full opportunity to start on your goal.

If you've always wanted to write a book, you could spend a few minutes each day, not more than 10 or 15 minutes, writing about your passion. With these few daily minutes, at the end of the year you would have a pretty significant book, likely over 300 pages.

What are the steps you need to take to reach your goal? If your project seems overwhelming or impossible, you haven't taken the time to "chunk" it down. Once you start on what seems like the most insignificant steps towards that which you desire, magical occurrences will begin to be revealed to you. I don't know how they occur, but it's true that when your "why" is strong enough, the "how" takes care of itself. Just when you need someone at a particular time, they magically appear. Remember the great law discovered by Sir Isaac Newton—an object in motion tends to stay in motion until acted upon by an outside force. By tackling the details of your goals one by one, you'll build momentum, self-esteem, an improved self-image, and, over time, your causes will produce your desired effects.

Step Eight:
Now Achieve That Goal—Take Action

> Go confidently in the direction of your dreams!
> Live the life you've imagined.
> –Henry David Thoreau

Measure Your Progress

Once you've gone through the previous seven steps, you're ready to measure your goal and ensure that it passes the final step.

Be Specific

Having "become more spiritual" on your list of goals can mean so many different things; it really is too vague. This particular goal might have come from your want list, and while there's nothing wrong with such vague or generalized goals, make sure you list an action plan for achieving a more spiritual state. For example, your action list could look like this:

- Book regular attendance at church in my calendar.
- Purchase a number of books that deal with the spiritual path I'd like to venture upon.
- Get together a group of like-minded people for dialogue and support.
- Look on the Internet for chat rooms that focus on my beliefs.

> All my life I've wanted to be someone;
> But I see now I should have been more specific.
> –Jane Wagner

Quantify and Qualify

Make sure that the specifics of your goals are aligned. Do you remember the example in chapter three where I asked you not to think of something? That's very difficult to do. Now, if I had said, think of something green, that at least starts to narrow the list down. And if I had further instructed you to think of something green, very small and hard, we've narrowed it down to a very short list.

Narrow your list down to the finest of details so your subconscious can go to work immediately with the specifics you've used to instruct it. If you want to earn more money in your career, be clear and refine your want to: "I want to earn $10,000 more per year in my career or other endeavours."

Alignment

Ensure your goal aligns with your greater purpose or vision in life.

Be Realistic

Is your goal realistic and are you willing to pursue it after you have run it through a cause/effect scenario?

Time Frames

Do you have a time frame in mind for reaching your goal? It's been said that there are no unrealistic goals, only unrealistic time frames. Do you want to earn ten times the amount of your current income? It is very likely that you can do it, but not necessarily in a year or two. It might, however, be an extremely realistic long-term goal that could be achieved in, perhaps, ten years or so. This is a great goal, but don't set yourself up for failure by creating an unrealistic time frame for achieving that goal.

Very few people ever think out their goals or work out how those goals should align with their life. As we know, very few people even write down their goals, period! How can you achieve anything if you don't even know what you're shooting for? If you asked your partner to go to the grocery store to purchase something, or a number of things, but didn't give a specific list of what to get, how likely is it that your home would be filled with the items you need? Highly unlikely, right? I know most women would consider themselves lucky if their partners came home with what they needed, even without a detailed list. So why would we expect that life would produce something we hadn't specifically asked for?

In conversations with my friends and clients who have not set goals, I've asked them why they haven't and I often get the same response. Either they feel that they'll be disappointed if they set a goal only to not achieve it, or they simply don't know what they want. They allow life to happen and then, on their thirtieth, fortieth, fiftieth, sixtieth, and seventieth birthdays, they either start to freak out or otherwise realize what they've missed out on.

Documentation

This is perhaps the most important part of goal setting: write, write, write. A "goals" journal is a great purchase that you could add to the $20 category in chapter four when you empty your piggy bank. By writing down your goals and working through them on paper, you'll further increase your likelihood of achieving them. Remember to update your goal book regularly with the process of this chapter and to celebrate your successes regularly.

Movie Magic – Become a Great Director

When was the last time you sat through a lousy movie and thought about what a waste of time and money it was? And when was the last time you went to a really terrible movie for the fifteenth time? Sound absurd? It is. So why do we choose to play the execrable scenes, pictures, and events in our minds over and over again. We have the greatest theatre of all time and have been given the job of director. All we need to do is learn how to run the projector of our mind for the most magical movies imaginable. Remember that your subconscious mind cannot tell the difference between a vividly imagined event and a real event.

Neuro-linguistic programming (NLP) provides tools for optimizing our movie-making abilities. NLP is a model of the best therapies and strategies of the past. It is a study of human excellence and is a powerful but practical approach to personal change. *Neuro* refers to our nervous system, the mental pathways of our five senses by which we see, hear, feel, taste and smell. *Linguistic* refers to our ability to use language and how specific words and phrases mirror our mental worlds. (Source: *NLP–The New Technology of Achievement* by Steve Andreas and Charles Faulkner.) *Programming* relates to our ability to configure our nervous system in a systematic way.

In NLP, we learn that there is a magical world within our mind that has the ability to play whatever movie it's trained to do. We can also improve on the images or movies we currently experience or dim and negate the images that we'd prefer not to re-experience or see.

Think of a positive experience right now. It doesn't have to be the greatest achievement of your life, just something that conjures positive thoughts, pictures, and feelings. What comes to mind? Is your picture or movie close to you in proximity or far away, black and white or in full and vibrant colour? Are the characters large or small, are you associated (seeing the picture from your own eyes) or are you disassociated (observing yourself participating in the experience)? What do you hear? Is there music playing? Are people speaking to you? If so, in what tone and how loudly or softly are they speaking? What are the feelings that you are experiencing in your body as you relive this experience?

We can use the above experience to further ingrain our goals into our consciousness and to make them more compelling and real. What did you experience from the paragraph above? Since it's a positive experience, many people will recall their pictures in colour, close proximity, and they were likely associated. If not, that's fine. Just take a few moments to write down what you had personally experienced:

_____

_____

_____

_____

_____

Let's assume that your goal is to go on vacation to Veradero, Cuba next year. I'll assume that you've already gone through all of the steps in this chapter to assure that this is the right goal for you within the next year, have written it down, and have done some research into Cuba and have a picture or two from the Internet or a travel brochure. To make this goal as compelling as possible and to ensure that your subconscious is in alignment with your conscious mind, we want to solidify this goal with a mini-movie.

Take a few moments to relax and close your eyes and imagine your trip. See it both through your own eyes and through disassociated eyes (as if you were filming yourself and the experience). Which one is more real and enjoyable for you? Stay in the more compelling view (associated or disassociated).

Now, imagine all of the shades of the perfect blue sky, the white silica sand, and the pristine, clear, teal-blue water. See the glistening stars that seem to dance off the water's surface with the slight warm breeze gently caressing your skin.

Next, change this picture or movie for a moment to that of black and white with shades of gray. Which felt better and more enjoyable to you? I'll guess it was the colour version.

Now make your picture as bright and close and large to you as possible. See it on an enormous big screen and you're sitting in the very front row. Now, slowly move your picture further and further into the horizon—or move to the back of the movie theatre and make the screen size smaller. I'll again guess that this does not feel as real as in the previous scenario.

In all of my suggestions above, I'll guess that when you did what I first asked, the picture of your vacation in Cuba seemed more realistic and plausible. You felt like you were there. I'll also guess that you stepped out of your daydream for a moment in the latter setting. These latter images might seem disappointing when you're focusing on what you want but they're extremely useful in changing the movie within your mind when you're stuck on what you don't want.

Let's use this simple strategy for alleviating something that might seem stressful or less than ideal. Think of a somewhat negative or anxiety-producing event in your past, but let's start with something relatively minor. I'll use an example of your having to confront someone at work who is somewhat intimidating to you. This person has been stealing all of your ideas and credit for your hard work and you think that reporting this to your boss will simply label you as a weak and vulnerable employee. You know you need to approach this person but it's not your style to confront situations such as these head on.

Try playing the movie of the above scenario in the following way. See the person that is intimidating you in your mind. They're likely to be large, above, and close to you. Try first changing the picture to black and white. Maybe even make your colleague wear some absurd article of clothing or perhaps they have some ketchup or mustard on their face from lunch. Imagine them moving further and further away from you in the picture of your mind and becoming smaller and smaller. Even try changing his or her voice to that of someone who has just inhaled from a helium balloon—almost like a cartoon character.

Now bring that small insignificant person back close to you. But for yourself, imagine that you keep growing bigger and bigger, taller and taller. You're so huge that when you look down at this person you need to confront, they're so tiny that if you moved your foot, you'd crush them like an ant. You almost pity your opponent now and look at them with new eyes as you're so strong and they're so small and weak. Do this several times, each time making improvements.

Now how do you feel about the person you need to confront? Do you feel a little more powerful and able to approach them without shaking in the knees? Keep running this type of movie for any apprehensive situation and you'll easily reduce the tension. Be creative. You're the director of this movie and can choose to create the compelling scene that works for you.

"Don't Get Your Hopes Up"

In speaking with friends and clients who have set only vague goals or who might be planning for an event, I discover that many have adopted a bizarre thought process when visualizing the outcome. When I ask about what's happening in their lives and they share with me something that could impact them positively in a wonderful way, they'll often quickly add, "Oh, but I don't want to get my hopes up." I've also been guilty of this, but I realized at an early age that it is a ridiculous notion.

The idea seems to be that if we don't get our hopes up, it won't hurt as badly when the event doesn't occur, or the disappointment will somehow be lessened because we have convinced ourselves that it doesn't matter if things do not go as planned. Or perhaps it's for social justification. So when a friend asks us about a goal that failed to work out, we can gracefully accept defeat because we hadn't got our hopes up.

I remember thinking logically about this absurd behaviour of my own and actually documented two events that I wanted very much to happen. In one instance I "got my hopes up" and was mentally committed to the event. With the other, I was much less involved and lied to myself that it didn't matter whether the event took place or not. What happened with respect to these two occurrences and my informal experiment? Much to my own surprise, I was equally disappointed in both cases regardless of my emotional engagement. I decided that if I was going to be disappointed anyway, wouldn't it make sense to be 100% engaged, especially if the disappointment wasn't going to be lessened by being 50% engaged? I had to question whether my lack of enthusiasm and visualization had led to the unsuccessful outcome. If I had poured my heart into it, could I have achieved my goal?

It's possible you've had an event or relationship or some other occurrence in your life where you have set yourself up to fail before even going after your goal, and we all get disappointed when something doesn't work out. This is the danger of measuring our merit in terms of our goals, as opposed to the person we have become on the journey towards our goals. Remember, it's the pursuit, not the end result.

Cheerleaders, Reality Checkers, and Dream Killers

> Friends are kind to each other's hopes.
> They cherish each other's dreams.
> –Henry David Thoreau

Be careful with whom you share your goals and dreams. Remember, first and foremost, your dreams are *yours*! They weren't created by or for the person you're sharing them with, so before you decide to make them public, keep that in mind. Don't expect the person to see your vision—it's yours. There are five things to consider when it comes to sharing this part of you:

1. Sharing opens up the opportunity for the person with whom you're sharing your dream to pass judgment. You might not even be fully convinced of your dream and could be quickly swayed by the opinion of this person. Why are you sharing with this person—for their approval, for praise?

> There are some decisions in life
> that only you can make.
> –Merle Shain

2. Just as Wayne Dyer warns us in *Manifest Your Destiny*, be aware of the "tribe" mentality. You probably belong to a tribe of some sort, either formally or informally. Generally, tribes have expectations for their members and set a certain ceiling for what can or cannot be accomplished. Tribes like to keep

their members in line. When you share your goals with your fellow tribe members, you run the risk of finding that your goal is above their ceiling.

> Great spirits have always encountered
> violent opposition from mediocre minds.
> –Albert Einstein

3. With whom are you sharing your goals? What type of person are they? Is it someone who knows more about the topic than you? Are you seeking another's advice and opinion in preference to your own? Is the person qualified to lead you? Are you just looking for someone who will listen to you? Perhaps you should seek the counsel of a support group. If your goal is to become a writer, for example, and your best friend is a very analytical dentist who hasn't read a book since university, what is your friend going to offer you in the way of advice? What does he know about being a writer? You would be better off joining a literary group or attending a workshop at the Writers Guild of Canada to find out about the challenges of becoming a writer.

> Risk more than others think is safe.
> Care more than others think is wise.
> Dream more than others think is practical.
> Expect more than others think is possible.
> –Claude Bissell

4. Listen to everyone and proceed with your heart. Everyone does have something valuable to say and contribute, despite the warnings in the previous point. Listen to everyone but distance yourself from that advice and then go along with your heart. It's better to fail in pursuing your dream than to succeed in doing what's not in your heart!

> Whether you think you can or whether
> you think you can't, you're right.
> –Henry Ford

5. Cheerleaders versus reality checkers—I have both of these individuals in my life. My mother has always been an obvious "cheerleader." No matter what crazy idea I dream up or how far out of reach it seems, my mom always cheers me on without the slightest hesitation or hint of analysis. My brother Dave, on the other hand, is a natural analytical thinker and "reality checker." His mind is so full of statistics that he can sometimes appear negative. Until just recently, I never really understood how both of these personality types could help me achieve my goals. I would often go to my mother when I needed an independent opinion about the validity of my goal and she would cheer me on even when I knew I wasn't ready to proceed. If I used my brother as a sounding board when I was starting off on a goal or brainstorming an idea, he would scare me so badly with "doom and gloom" scenarios and the number of things that might go wrong that I wouldn't even start on the task for fear of a catastrophic failure.

Both my mom and brother are capable of reacting in very different ways from this normal pattern. My mom will often comment on some critical flaw she has observed before I set out toward a goal, and my brother does show cheerleading traits when he sees that my goal has the potential to become a reality. But, for the most part, my mom is my cheerleader and my brother Dave is my reality checker. So why not use them to my advantage?

Generally speaking, I always brainstorm my dreams and goals with my mom. She puts me up on such a high pedestal that no obstacle seems insurmountable after five minutes with her. Then, when I've nearly attained my goal, I enlist the opinion of Dave, as I know he will point out plans B to Z and provide protection strategies that will allow me to plan in advance for possible obstacles. Recognize these different support people in your own life, and use their natural strategies for greater support just when you need it. The cheerleaders and the reality checkers see and evaluate goals and dreams differently. Keep this in mind when you decide to share your visions.

Become a Student of Life

After we've finished school, so many of us give up being a student. I remember reading somewhere that a large percentage of people never read another book after high school or college. We might take a course or two, attend lectures and possibly upgrade our degrees, but few people are true students of life. Why reinvent the wheel when you can model the successful people and the achievements of others and learn their secrets in a fraction of the time?

> Learning is not attained by chance, it must be sought
> for with ardor and attended to with diligence.
> –Abigail Adams

When I first started my career in the financial planning industry, I was only an eighteen-year-old girl in a world of gray-haired men with decades of experience. I didn't have the first clue of what success meant to my current or future clients, let alone what it meant to me.

We had a branch meeting one day and one of the investment companies that our firm dealt with sent an energetic lad from England to impart some marketing wisdom our way. My seasoned associates attended but turned a deaf ear to this fellow's outrageous and passionate ideas. I was totally enthralled with the notions presented and acted upon one immediately. This man gave the suggestion of contacting all of the powerful business people in our city with a letter. The letter was to request a brief meeting to discover what specifically made them successful. It was to be a fact-finding meeting only and not one intended on selling any product or service.

After our workshop, I immediately headed back to my office, dug out my chamber of commerce directory and quickly highlighted the companies and owners that I knew were successful in my city. I drafted a letter and sent it out to over fifty of these prominent presidents and company owners. I decided to follow up with a phone call, as I didn't hear from a single person nearly two weeks after sending the letters. This was an extremely uncomfortable process for me but I figured that the worst thing that could happen when I called and requested a meeting was for them to say no. I recall that I received an invitation to meet with seven business owners at their offices. I had my interview questions ready and interviewed all owners with delight and enthusiastic wonder.

My first question for each interview was, "What has made you successful?" To my surprise, each and every person stammered and paused a little and assured me that they were not all that successful. How could this be? I knew they were successful. They were written about and interviewed regularly by the press and had the recognition of almost everyone in the city. How could they not think of themselves as successful?

My intensive questioning provided me with some useful models of success, was enlightening, and, at the end of each interview, I did learn many of the secret ingredients to a successful life as defined differently by each person. I also found that each interviewee felt a little more successful after they had verbalized their achievements to someone truly wanting to learn about them and who actively listened. I took away a number of invaluable insights, made contacts with some of the most affluent people in my city, and left feeling edified by the end of our meeting. A classic win-win situation.

> Learning is not compulsory...neither is survival.
> –W. Edwards Deming

Become a student of life as I did and do so for a lifetime. Start by observing your friends, family, and associates. What do they do very well and how can you learn from them? Do you have a friend that is an outstanding mother that can multitask with ease and efficiency? Do you also have a friend that you find is a money management master? You might be surprised that a long-time friend or family member that you thought you really knew has more to share than you ever imagined, and it's just a few questions away. The key to a successful interview is great listening skills. Remember that you're not there to share or relate anything about yourself. The purpose of your interview is to use a Socratic approach to identify the equation or recipe for success in that person's life. Furthermore, you'll benefit the interviewee by allowing them to acknowledge what they've done well in life and affirm their achievements.

Summary

- How do you define success? Have you set yourself up to win by examining the rules for playing a successful game?
- The only thing you might have in common with a billionaire is that you both have the same 24 hours in a day. Use them wisely.
- Set realistic goals and measure them against your values list and the higher purpose that you've created for your life, then use the law of cause and effect to determine if your goals are worthy of you.
- Live passionately and give your all every day. Get your hopes up!

• Keep your dreams confidential and share them cautiously.

Your Prosperity Action Steps

• Have you defined what success specifically means to you? Write your personal mission statement and all that success entails for you.

• Type or write out the daily success formula and for thirty days, tape it to your bathroom mirror. Also, detail an action plan based on each of the factors within the equation. What will you do to expand your level of appreciation and focus? And what strategies will you employ and when?

• What one thing will you do each week to more effectively use the 24 hours you've been given? Could you wake up an hour earlier, watch one less hour of television, or perhaps multitask and learn something new from an audio program while completing some mundane task? For instance, you could listen to an interesting audio book in your car while you are driving to work.

• Re-read the beginning of this chapter and set your goals on paper today!

• Practice becoming a better movie director at least once this week. Even better, you could spend 10 minutes each morning and evening vividly playing a movie of a goal that you want to achieve.

• Book an appointment with your friends and family. Write down all of the individuals that you know and what they could teach you. Also find out who they know and see if you would like to meet them. Call or e-mail them this week and ask for a brief interview. Remember to become a student of life!

Chapter Six
Fear Factor

State Management – Use Your Brain for a Change

Personal state management is perhaps one of the most important tools I would like to share with you. People who can focus on what they want and then take the appropriate and necessary actions certainly have a much better chance at achieving their goals and dreams. But what about those days that you just don't feel like going after anything? There are days when just getting out of bed seems like a colossal chore. How does one hope to master life if getting out of bed is a monumental task?

Understanding what controls your mental state and then improving upon these conditions will make getting up in the morning and all of life's other challenges more exciting and empowering.

Studies have been conducted on countless people that have reported chronic depression. Think of someone you know that's depressed or a time that you've experienced feelings of intense malaise. Look at that person's posture, their stance, their shallow breathing, where their eyes focus, all the while making gray, lifeless, and disempowering pictures or movies in their mind's eye, and we quickly learn that physiology is the first key in state management. If a person is slumped over, speaks slowly and with little to no life or passion, and primarily stares at the floor while accessing their feelings, how could they not feel lethargic and depressed? Experience that setting just for a moment and couple that with a number of depressing thoughts.

Now, stand up, clap your hands loudly, speak forcefully, or jump around for a minute. Take a few moments to appreciate what you have in life, whom you love, and what you love to do, and all of the opportunities that await you in the future.

Does this second exercise feel a little better than the first? Does your body feel stronger and your mind a bit more focused?

State management consists of a number of areas of focus and application. What you put into your body, how and how much you move your body, what you focus your attention on, and a number of environmental factors can put you on top of the world or in the doldrums of despair.

You Are What You Eat

> Tell me what you eat,
> and I will tell you what you are.
> –Anthelme Brillat-Savarin

How you think, act, and even learn is affected greatly by what types of food you eat. A variety of foods are reputed to affect our moods and brain chemistry. Many individuals on low-fat carbohydrate-restricted diets report increased feelings of depression, grumpiness, frustration, and malaise.

Conversely, when we head to mom's for a big Sunday dinner or opt for a steaming plate of pasta or mash potatoes, we usually characterize such food as "comfort food." Can food really change our brain chemistry and our moods? Current research is telling us just that.

Does reaching for your favourite chocolate treat send you into an immediate state of satisfaction and bliss? There's a reason that chocolate is desirable almost universally. There are a host of substances found in chocolate that are cited as being responsible for mood-altering and mood-lifting effects. Researchers believe that chocolate alters mood primarily by causing the release of endorphins, the brain's opiates.

Know Your Aminos

There are two important amino acids contained in proteins that greatly affect your brain chemistry and can result in positive or negative moods. Both tryptophan and tyrosine are responsible for influencing the production of the neurotransmitter (brain chemical) serotonin.

Serotonin is the neurotransmitter that relaxes the brain. The other three, collectively known as catecholamines, are neurotransmitters that rev up the brain. Turkey and chicken contain tryptophan and when converted to serotonin, give us that "good" feeling. Carbohydrate cravings might be a subconscious attempt to raise serotonin levels, which is responsible for mood, sleep, and appetite control. (Source: Dr. Bill Sears. "Best Brain Foods: 11 Ways Food Can Help You Think." www.askdrsears.com.)

Researchers at Brookhaven National Laboratory have shown that looking at our favourite fat-laden foods makes the brain release dopamine, the chemical associated with reward and craving. Physiologist Mary Dallman at the University of California, San Francisco says that fat and sugar calm the brain, lowering levels of stress hormones; "That's why we call them comfort foods," she says. Vitamins and minerals are also essential good-mood nutrients, including vitamin B6, vitamin C, folic acid, and zinc. They're further needed to support the production of serotonin in producing the necessary brain chemistry. (Source: Anne Underwood. "That's Why We Call It Junk Food." *Newsweek* online, 2006.)

For more information on foods that rev up and slow down our brains, visit www.thewomansguidetomoney. com for a complete list and other valuable facts.

The more severe the pain or illness, the more severe
will be the necessary changes. These may involve
breaking bad habits, acquiring some new and better ones.
–Peter McWilliams

Your Environment Has Power

Which would you prefer as an ideal workday? Choice A involves taking your laptop and a briefcase full of files to the beach or spending your workday outside in nature on a warm breezy day with your iPod playing Pachabel or your favourite calming music. Choice B involves working in a tower full of electromagnetic disturbances, recycled air, fluorescent lights, and a barrage of humming and other annoying noises. Your choice is likely A or something similar. Why? We know that a peaceful and relaxing environment can induce an optimal atmosphere for creativity. Understanding your unique sensitivities to sounds, sights and feelings will increase your chances for exemplary brainpower and physical states.

Music, whether at work or at home, can produce an instant change of state. If you have teenagers or young nieces and nephews, you can relate to the instant state change that can occur when their sometimes nerve-wracking music is too loud or has pounding bass. Conversely, when dining at an elegant restaurant or indulging in a service at your favorite spa, it's no secret that they use specific music to enhance the relaxation response. Music is also an inexpensive and effortless means to reducing disturbing background noises to focus our auditory attention on the pleasant.

Fear Factor

Fear and worry are conditions that can be downright debilitating. While state management and the above techniques will support the brain function and physiology for handling fear and anxiety, more attention is required to overcome these abrasive grinding emotions. The following is a simple seven-step process for handling and controlling fear, worry, and anxiety.

> Of all the liars in the world, sometimes
> the worst are your own fears.
> –Rudyard Kipling

Seven Steps to Overcoming Worry and Handling Fear

I've heard that more people die on Monday morning between 8 and 9 a.m. than at any other time; people are literally dying to go to work. But what holds you and me back from living a life of joy come Monday morning? Fear of "unknown hells versus unknown heavens," as Deepak Chopra so eloquently puts it in *A Path to Love*. This worry and fear of the unknown has become so widespread that job dissatisfaction is now considered to be the number one source of heart disease! It's not what you're eating that will kill you, it's what's eating into you!

So what's stopping us as a society from doing the brave thing and pursuing our dream jobs? Bravery presupposes acting in spite of fear and doubt. Does this all sound too esoteric for your Monday morning?

I love the serenity prayer of Reinhold Niebuhr where he states so simply and eloquently the rightful place for worry:

> God grant me the serenity
> To accept the things I cannot change,
> Courage to change the things I can,
> And the wisdom to know the difference.

Really, there are only two types of worries: Those that you can't do anything about (so why worry about them?), and those that you do have control over and can change (if you can change them, change them).

Step One:
Schedule Worry

Why not? We seem to schedule everything else these days. We schedule soccer practice for the kids, a meeting with the designer who will help us with our furniture purchase, or with the travel agent so we can plan our next vacation. Why wouldn't we schedule something that so many of us spend countless hours doing? If worry is at least booked, we can focus on it fully.

We all know that most of what we worry about rarely comes true and will result in a negative frame of mind, so why on earth would we book it in to our lives and on a regular basis? I'm proposing that you try this little exercise for just 15 to 20 minutes each week. I guarantee that's less time than you would spend on the worries that seep into your consciousness throughout the day on a normal week. As worrisome thoughts creep up on you, pull out a sticky note or a receipt slip from your wallet or purse and write down your worry. Then *forget it*! Just let it go until your scheduled time to recommence your worrying.

The first benefit of this exercise is distance. By the time your "worry" appointment arrives, the intensity of your worry hopefully will have lessened, even if only by a microscopic amount. Second, in a nation where most of us list procrastination as a major fault, this should be as simple as pie—put it off until later.

> Do not anticipate trouble, or worry about
> what may never happen. Keep in the sunlight.
> –Benjamin Franklin

Steps for Overcoming Worry

Take a blank sheet of paper and list all of the problems that cause you worry or feelings of anxiety or fear. Identify your top three worries, and on a second sheet of paper, write out all the possible solutions for solving your problems. This is not an easy task and might take a few days, or even weeks, to complete. Add to your "worries" list if new ones arise but keep tackling them as you go. The exercise of writing out your worries takes them out of your head and allows you to look at them and check their validity.

As you work through your worries and possible solutions to them, here are a few strategies that might assist you in the process:

First, *check your physical and mental states*. In order to develop your solutions list, it's imperative that you be at your best both mentally and physically. If you're slumped over on the sofa, staring at the floor, and wondering how you're ever going to get that raise to help pay for the cost of Mary's university education, you are not in any sort of position to solve your problem. Stand or sit up, take some deep and empowering breaths, run a few laps around the house, smile stupidly at yourself in the mirror, read a few funnies in your local newspaper. Basically, do anything it takes to shake off a less-than-ideal mood before you can expect your creative juices to flow. If you're still not sure about what to do, act "as if" and ask yourself the following question: "If I were a (insert the adjective of your choice here: creative, confident, passionate, etc.) person, how would I sit, stand, breath and tackle this problem?"

Second, *try solving someone else's problem.* Have you ever found that it's amazingly easy to discover solutions when friends confide in you about problems they have? If you're like me, you will probably find many creative solutions for another person's problems because you're not emotionally attached to the issues. Try picturing your challenge and putting it far in front of you mentally. Now, pretend it's a friend's issue. This is a great time to bring out your imaginary friend from childhood, if you were blessed enough to have one. Pretend it's someone else's problem and distance yourself from it emotionally and see what solutions arise.

Last, ask yourself, *"What's the worst that can happen?"* This is an empowering question. We often worry about some event that might or might not happen, or anxiety builds in us about a project or some other obsession. What if your project doesn't turn out to be perfect? What if that relationship is over? What if you do lose your job? What's the worst thing that can happen? Will you die? Probably not. Will you starve and be thrown out into the streets? Again, most unlikely. If you can handle the worst that could happen and take a quick moment to picture the thing that you fear, you might find that it's not that bad and this knowledge will bring a sense of ease to the current tasks at hand.

Go Big or Go Home

In the same way that you schedule worry, schedule other emotions too. Sometimes it's just not possible to do so in advance as the emotion sometimes needs to be fully felt and everything else must stop. We fool ourselves into thinking that we'll just ignore an intense emotion, keep going through our day, and deal with it later. Just stop and take a 30-minute break. Trust me, you're going to waste much more time if you hold on, all day long, to an emotion that isn't serving you. Feel it fully—but put a limit on it.

If you're feeling angry, look up that word, and every similar word, and then go for a walk and mumble all of those words to yourself. Work yourself up for a time—maybe 20 to 30 minutes—and get out all of that anger. Then, when you walk back into your house or office, it's done. You have experienced it fully and you don't need it to linger any longer.

It might take a few times to get the hang of this method but I promise that you'll feel more satisfied as a result. After a while, you won't need 20 minutes either; you'll find that you can fully experience the negative feeling and emotion in a few minutes and then move on, with the lesson learned.

It's like eating those low-fat cookies. You're craving sugar and chocolate and somehow you convince yourself that eating low-fat cookies with half the fat, but often with as many calories as the regular versions, will satisfy your cravings. What usually happens? If you're like me, after you've eaten the entire bag and are still craving more, you realize that just a couple of the regular cookies would have satisfied you. Don't be fooled into suppressing emotions or letting them linger all day. Have a few fatty treats, experience a full-out temper tantrum if necessary but do it alone and in a respectful manner and feel more satisfied at the end of the day.

We live in what I like to call a "suppression society." Emotionally, physically, and spiritually we fall into the trap where society forces its "get over it" attitude upon us. We fill up with emotional toxins and are shocked when they manifest into diseases, mental illnesses, or mid-life crises.

William Blake, a British poet, painter, and visionary, eloquently reminds us that suppression can be lethal in his poem entitled *A Poison Tree*:

> I was angry with my friend:
> I told my wrath, my wrath did end.
> I was angry with my foe;
> I told it not, my wrath did grow.
>
> And I water'd it in fears,
> Night & morning with my tears;
> And I sunned it with my smiles,
> And with soft deceitful wiles.
>
> And it grew both day and night,
> Till it bore an apple bright,
> And my foe beheld it shine,
> And he knew that it was mine,
>
> And into my garden stole
> When the night had veil'd the pole:
> In the morning glad I see
> My foe outstretch'd beneath the tree.

Centuries later, the words of William Blake still ring true and carry the same relevance of communicating our true feeling, not just "sunning them with our smiles."

In this suppression society, people with colds, flu, and emotional and physical aches and pains drag themselves to work instead of healing themselves first and worrying about work second. If a family member dies, we're lucky to get a couple of days off work and then we'd better be ready to hit the ground running the first day back because we've got to make up for lost time, right? And breaking up with the love of your life? We'd better get over that one quickly, it's not in the company manual and it certainly doesn't qualify for a day off. We'd be lucky if we get a drink out with a friend to talk about the heartbreak.

You can start now, with yourself, and demand that your work and your world support the normal processes of living and dealing with physical, emotional, and spiritual challenges. Continuing to work as you try to deal with the issues will only lengthen the time it takes to recover. If your boss can't appreciate that as a healthy and whole person you are a more efficient worker, maybe it's time to find a new job. If you are your own boss, then it's time to have a chat with yourself. You will have time when you retire, lose your job, take an extended vacation, but who will you be then? As Wayne Dyer so cogently states in *Manifest Your Destiny*: "If you are what you do, then what are you when you don't?"

> Courage is the art of being the only one
> that knows you're scared to death.
> –Harold Wilson

Step Two:
Feel the Fear and Do It Anyway

In her book *Feel the Fear and Do It Anyway*, Susan Jeffers answers a question that had plagued me for many years. She states that everyone is fearful so our goal shouldn't be to eliminate fear, but to be aware of it, feel it, and "do it anyway." I regret that I didn't read this book when I was fresh out of school, as it would have made my angst about my fear more palatable and, by doing that, would have presented me with more choices.

In the financial world, in which I have chosen to work for over a decade, public speaking is a part of the job. This simple task of speaking in front of others happens to be close to the number one fear for many North Americans and I am no exception.

Early in my career, anxiety would haunt me for weeks ahead of a talk, regardless of the size of the audience. Speaking in public, however, was necessary for my advancement and to procure further business for my firm, so opting out wasn't an option. Furthermore, I felt fantastic after each lecture because I had *faced* my fear, but as soon as my next talk was booked, I knew I hadn't *conquered* my fear. When I was nervous before a talk, and often one step away from a full-blown anxiety attack, I blamed my lack of experience for my inability to control my nerves. Over time, I have become a tiny bit more comfortable in front of an audience and it certainly helps to know my material. If several talks are booked close together, I get "used to" the pressure.

Nearly twelve years later in my career, the nerves are still there, and if I haven't spoken for some time, the anxiety is nearly as great as it was when I gave my first talk. I couldn't understand how hundreds of talks later, given to thousands of people and with the knowledge from their feedback that my message was important and well-received, my fear could follow me. Why, after years of public-speaking courses and personal coaching, couldn't I just get up on stage naturally with a successful end in mind?

> Be kind, for everyone you
> meet is fighting a hard battle.
> –Plato

I think a job interview can be an intimidating and fearful experience for most interviewees. I certainly have had my share over the years and, just as with my lectures, it didn't matter how many I had, the nerves always followed me to each interview. It always felt daunting to be on the opposite side of the table from someone so confident and calm, who asked question after question in an effort to determine if I was worthy of that company.

Finally, a year after I opened my own company, it was

my turn to be the interviewer. And to my surprise, I was as nervous as I used to be when I was the interviewee. I was shocked! All of those years I had focused on my own fear and insecurity going into the interview process and never once did I stop to think that the person on the other side of the table, who seemed so intimidating, might have been just as nervous as I was. Now that my turn had come to put question after question to potential staff members, I wondered how I came across as an employer, whether my queries were the norm, and so on.

After I read *Feel the Fear and Do It Anyway*, it all became so clear. The fear might never disappear, but that shouldn't be our focus. The challenge is to feel our fear but to do the task anyway. It's so simple and calming to know that we all have fears. Take the time to share your fears with others and they'll likely share theirs with you. Also take the time to read or watch television biographies of those individuals you respect. You might find out that no matter how mighty that person seems, he or she probably has a list of fears as long as yours.

> Don't waste yourself in rejection, nor bark against
> the bad, but chant the beauty of the good.
> –Ralph Waldo Emerson

Step Three:
Do the Opposite and Focus on What You Want

It's been said that if drivers who lose control of their cars and are facing an imminent crash would keep their eyes on the road in the direction they want to go, and not on the collision path, they'd have a much better chance of avoiding an accident. Face the direction you'd like to head in, and not towards that collision course. And be very cautious about the words you speak and those that others say to you. Words can be as sweet as honey or like thought viruses that seep deep into your subconscious.

Society is full of thought viruses that we've conditioned

our nervous system to accept. A mother lovingly cautions her child, "Don't spill the milk" or "Don't fall" as little Johnny is running. What she doesn't realize is she's giving little Johnny's subconscious a command. The subconscious doesn't understand negatives, so when a person says, "don't fall," the mind has to picture falling and the focus is therefore on falling. Is that the reason Johnny has been falling lately?

Do you remember the example in chapter three where I asked you not to think of the colour blue? How difficult was that? So it would be far better for the loving and concerned mother to command the nervous system of her child with a positive and focusing statement such as "Please be careful when running, Johnny." It's funny, but it works with us big kids too!

So when the time comes to worry about your bills, for example, why not think about all of the income-generating possibilities you have if you just use the gold mine between your ears? What if, instead of worrying about whether you'll ever get married or have children or start that family you've always wanted, you do something totally different yet ridiculously simple? You grab your pen and a blank sheet of paper and begin to write down all of the possible ways you could meet the spouse of your dreams. Many of your ideas might not amount to anything but even if you think of a few good ones or run it by a personal support group for further input, you're now availing yourself of solutions that likely would not have arisen out of your previous self-pity and worry.

> Courage is knowing what not to fear.
> –Plato

Try this mental exercise for a moment. Close your eyes and imagine going up the tallest building you can imagine. You're riding the elevator all the way up many, many storeys to the roof of the building. Now walk over to the edge, stand with your toes slightly over the edge of the building, and look down. Now, slowly back away from the edge, or crawl if you must. How did this little exercise make you feel? The first time I tried it, I felt slightly lightheaded and I'm not fearful of heights in the least. But consider this for a moment: it was all in your mind. You weren't actually on that building's roof looking over the edge. You were sitting in your office or home safe and sound. Generally speaking, unless someone is physically threatening us and death is imminent, it's unlikely that our worry is going to kill us. So remember to step off the ledge in your mind and see worry for what it really is: all in our minds!

Step Four:
Remember What You've Overcome Before

> Courage is resistance to fear, mastery of fear—
> not absence of fear.
> –Mark Twain

When my brother returned from an extended trip to Egypt some time ago, I remember being fascinated by his stories of the missing pieces of Egypt's past. He indicated that ancient Egyptian historians did not include any reports of massive failures or defeats. They just wouldn't write about it. I thought this was quite brilliant indeed— don't report it and it didn't happen! I would *not* like you to act as the Egyptians but to actively work to remember your failures. Our failures help us in so many ways.

An accounting of failures will help you overcome challenges. When you take the time to recall what you've been through, you then have a list of "compared to what?" items. Once you have prepared this account and compared some of your current worries against it, I'm quite confident that you will think: "This is silly! Why am I worrying about this? If I could overcome [insert great challenge from the past here], why am I concerned with this? Compared to what I've overcome, I can certainly handle this."

I'm not suggesting that you go to great lengths to recall the past or to live in it for any length of time, just recall and record some major challenges—the ones that ended successfully and, unlike our ancient Egyptian friends, those that didn't. But, more important, make a list of what you have learned, the sort of person you have become because of the experience, and the challenges you overcame.

My story is one of missed opportunity, but certainly not one of regret. In my middle teen years, I was presented with a once-in-a-lifetime chance to work in New York City as a model. All of my friends and most of my family insisted that the decision warranted no debate or hesitation—it's New York City. I had to go because everyone was telling me I should.

The story is long but entailed all of the preparation that goes with a long-distance move, including closing bank accounts and countless sobbing sessions with my mom and other friends.

What I didn't realize at the time, as I was only starting to work on the values and priorities in my life, was that family would always be more important to me than a career opportunity or, better put, the pursuit of money. I didn't want to be a model and I loved my family, especially my best friend—my mother. Why was I leaving the most important part of my life behind for a job I loathed? So, within 24 hours of my departure, and after thousands of tears shed later by my mom and myself, I returned home to great relief and love.

Most of you are probably thinking: come on, New York? What's so tough about that? Nothing, I suppose, but for me it meant leaving everything my life stood for at the time for something that meant nothing to me and in which my heart was not fully engaged. I learned a valuable lesson at an early age: measuring your decisions against your true values early on in the process will save you a lot of pain and deliberation. Every time my mom and I live through a rough challenge together, I always say the same thing (even though it's now many years later), "At least we have each other and I'm not in New York." My mom then gives a huge sigh of relief as she remembers that, for us, the ultimate gift is our time together.

Remembering our past challenges provides a wonderful gift that is full of surprises and lessons to hold on to. The lessons might be simple or profound, but I encourage you to take a few minutes each week to remember what you've been through. Answers to what you're now going through will magically reveal themselves.

Step Five:
Come from a Spirit of Gratitude, Appreciation, and Love

Embrace a kind and giving spirit towards yourself. This is one of the simplest and most effortless tasks you can perform. You can do it anywhere, any time, and in an instant! Keep that elastic band on as we discussed in the 30-day challenge and banish fear and worry by taking a few moments to be grateful—it will shift your entire frame of mind and, more important, your life. The world is a magical place and I'm always amazed at how quickly life will snap its elastic band on me when I begin to pity myself.

I can't tell you how many times I've been driving or walking somewhere, totally absorbed in my own problems, with even perhaps a little "poor me" attitude, and then, almost in an instant, someone will cross my path and make me take a gasp—someone who's blind, homeless, or with more challenges than I have. This awakens me from my self-absorption and brings on thoughts of love, gratefulness, and appreciation for all of life. These occurrences are as predictable for me as the sun rising; when I feel sorry for myself, the world shows me why I should be grateful for all that I have.

Some things to be grateful for could include the car you drive to make a journey that used to take people days or weeks to travel, the running water you've never thought twice about, or the medical advancements that have added significantly to our lives and that were unknown just a few short decades ago.

Do you know how many people in the world would give anything to come to this country—to live free anywhere in North America? To be free is such a wonderful gift that they would gladly take our worst day. So the next time you're feeling down in the dumps and wish you had "that guy's life" or "that girl's life," remember the billions of people worldwide who would like to have *your* life!

Step Six:
Develop a Positive Support Group

> You can never solve a problem
> on the level on which it was created.
> –Albert Einstein

Initially, this step might just involve you and your journal or a blank pad of paper, but I strongly suggest that you gather a group of like-minded individuals who have the common goal of periodically getting together to discuss solutions for each other's challenges. This need not be a formal or even a large gathering—two will do just fine.

Einstein, being the smart guy that he was, basically tried to tell us that if we created a problem, how could we, by ourselves, see a way out of that problem? This is where a group of your non-judgmental friends may decide to meet a few times a year to discuss issues that need additional introspection. We so often chat at a very superficial level with our friends. How are the kids? And work is still going fine, is it? Although deep issues might be troubling us, sometimes without our conscious mind even realizing it, we fail to reach out for some independent analysis.

If you're blessed enough to have some listeners in your life, and not just solution providers, this approach could prove most worthwhile. It allows you to set the stage to dissect and analyze each other's problems in a non-judgmental way that isn't geared towards providing solutions. You don't want to risk following the advice of someone you shouldn't. The idea is to engage in dialogue about your problem and have the other person (or people) help you to identify more creative solutions.

Now, I will caution you that sometimes you might not be able to find a group or even an individual to fill this role, and then your best friend might very well be a book. Try befriending some excellent authors and use them as guides to self-discovery.

Look for a solution model. Do you know anyone who has solved a problem similar to yours? Perhaps your answer is as close as a bookstore, the Internet, or a phone call to a good friend. Use the experiences of others to help solve your problems. You might find great comfort in sharing your experiences with a stranger in an Internet chat room or a local live support group. Learning how others solved the problems you're facing will bring encouragement and confidence that you too will be able to overcome your challenge.

Finally, know when to seek outside help. Although friends and family members can be a wonderful resource in the search for solutions to many problems, there are times when your immediate peer group has limited expertise or is unable to provide what you are looking for. Sometimes you need to seek the counsel of a professional trained in psychology or psychiatry or even a local support group. You might also need the professional help of experts in other fields. Try taking a course in an area that could improve your qualifications and abilities and thus banish any feelings of incompetence.

While developing a positive support group, you might realize that you already have a support group no matter how large or small. It might consist of only a spouse, or add a number of friends and family members. As wonderful as these groups and the support they lend to us throughout our lifetimes are, the tribal consciousness, as it were, needs to be examined periodically.

We explored a fraction of what our peer group can cause us to believe as true and absolute in chapter two when we examined thought viruses. But how about social norms? Have you put any thought into what your peer group considers a social norm and what another group might consider as totally acceptable or unacceptable? For example, why do we tip at a restaurant?

The word *tip* has its origins as a seventeenth-century thieves' cant word for "to pass on." People have also turned the word into an acronym that stands for "[T]o [I]nsure [P]romptness." Russell Roberts, an economist at Washington University in St. Louis has found that no one knows for sure why most North Americans tip at a restaurant, and he has some interesting conclusions on the matter. Roberts suggests that people frequently use social rules of thumb when interacting with each other, without conscious acknowledgement, as a way to make life a more pleasant experience. Another example is how we will wait in line at a grocery store or movie rather than pushing our way to the front of the line.

So how can the acceptance of these social norms affect our ability to attract wealth and abundance or simply to lead a happier and more peaceful life? If we adopt the beliefs, behaviours, and norms of our peer groups without conscious introspection, we could be in trouble.

Money Memories Can Harm Your Relationships

During the time I owned my own financial planning firm, I had two clients who were a very astute couple. They were in their forties when I met them and had done very well for themselves. They married late in life and had been together for only a few years. They each had over a hundred thousand dollars in savings, had great pension plans, and were debt free including a mortgage.

"Janet" was a conscientious investor and always had a

list of questions for me when we met. She was one of my most challenging clients and I enjoyed how she would always test me. "Gary" was very laid back and knew that Janet loved researching anything to do with their finances. Most of the time, Gary wouldn't even come along to our meetings.

Janet was the Olympic athlete of investing. She always spent less than she made, she had a healthy "emergency" account, and worked hard in life and her career to pay off all of her debts early. Sadly, during our discussions, Janet always needed an unusual reassurance that she would be financially sound in her retirement. She never felt that she had enough and was terrified to spend money on herself or on anything non-essential like a vacation or new furniture for their home.

Janet informed me that she thought she might one day be a "bag lady" and her greatest fear was that this day could arrive in her retirement. It was an obsession of hers to do as much as she could now to ensure that this didn't happen to her. We discussed her fear openly and she admitted that it wasn't logical. We future-valued her investments and pension plan and she agreed that there would be more than enough for her at retirement even based on very conservative investing, yet this did nothing to assuage her fear

Janet was raised in a wealthy family, but the average person wouldn't know it. Her grandparents lived with her mother and father during her childhood and the entire family subscribed to a poverty consciousness. After a lot of dialogue over the years with Janet, she shared with me that her grandparents, who were a big influence on her young life, grew up in the Depression. They had lost everything during those years. It was tough on them and a short time later, they arrived in Canada. Although the average person would consider the wealth they amassed thereafter a fortune, Janet's grandparents didn't. They still scrimped and saved and feared the day when it would again all be lost.

Does this sound a little like Bob in chapter one?

Janet and Gary had a great marriage. They didn't have children at the time, had exciting and fulfilling careers and generally got along. There was, however, a severe point of contention that the average person might scoff at. Numerous times each week, Gary and Janet would fight about food. Of all of the problems an average couple has to face, theirs was about food.

As a person that abhorred waste, Janet insisted on finishing leftovers the day after. Gary despised this notion. They made more than enough money to eat "fresh" food each day. He wasn't a wasteful person either but he didn't feel that he deserved to eat second-rate servings the day after.

Week after week, and just about every second day, the fight continued throughout the years. The real issue? Gary grew up in a very impoverished household. His mother was a single parent of four and rarely had enough food on the table for all of them. Should there be any excess from dinner, certainly leftovers would be devoured the next night. Gary vowed that when he was an adult, he would *never* have to eat leftovers again. Unfortunately, Gary had never specifically articulated this declaration to Janet and she hadn't made it clear to him why it was so important that they not waste food.

Once this realization was finally discussed openly between them, they had a new understanding of their childhood and of what was very important to them as adults. Now once in a while, Gary eats leftovers and Janet has eased up on cooking excess food and forcing Gary to eat it. Their arguments have stopped and they now speak freely when financial issues arise.

What's more important is that Janet started to seriously play the Five Bank Account system. She always excelled with finances but still had this nagging "bag lady" fear and an inability to spend on herself without guilt. After three months of playing the banking game and seeing the funds accumulate in her financial independence account, she knew that she could never be a bag lady; this account wouldn't let her. She also reported immediate success with the purchases account and found a new freedom and security with her money.

Janet had so much fun with her accounts that Gary even joined in after the six-month mark. He had initially called me the first month complaining that I made his wife open all of these accounts, but once he played for a few months, he happily called back and apologized for his oversight.

Peer Assessment Questionnaire
Where Did Your Peers Come From?

If Janet and Gary had taken a few moments at the start of their relationship to examine where their money beliefs had originated, perhaps they never would have argued about such trivial things as leftovers. Take time to learn the pasts of your spouse and peers. This way, when they exhibit a trait that perplexes you, you'll be better prepared to help people around you overcome their potentially obstructive habits.

1. What were your spouse's/peer's earliest thoughts about money?

_____

_____

_____

2. What were your spouse's/peer's early positive memories and experiences with money?

_____

_____

_____

3. What was your spouse's/peer's first limiting or negative memory or experience with money?

_____

_____

_____

4. Did your spouse's/peer's parents have a sufficient amount of money?

_____

_____

_____

5. If your spouse's/peer's parents had money problems, what were they? (i.e. not enough money, spent all of their money, were not able to spend their money, etc.)

_____

_____

_____

6. What did your spouse/peer experience from their parents' money problems?

_____

_____

_____

7. What positive learning experiences did your spouse/peer gain from their parents regarding money and wealth?

_____

_____

_____

8. What did your spouse/peer learn *not to do* from their parents regarding money and wealth?

_____

_____

_____

9. During their childhood and adolescent years, what did your spouse/peer learn from their peer groups about having money?

_____

_____

_____

10. During this period, what did your spouse/peer think of wealthy people?

_____

_____

_____

11. What did your spouse/peer *not* have growing up?

_____

_____

_____

12. What did social groups teach your spouse/peer about money and wealth? (i.e. religious groups, social clubs, etc.)

_____

_____

_____

13. What core beliefs does your spouse/peer remember growing up regarding money and wealth? (i.e. money is easy to earn; you only get money and ahead at the expense of others, etc.)

_____

_____

_____

14. Did your spouse/peer have a piggy bank or a secret storage place for their money? What was it? What did it look like?

_____

_____

_____

15. What did your spouse/peer purchase when they would empty their piggy bank?

_____

_____

_____

16. Where did your spouse/peer get money from when they were a child? (i.e. allowance, birthday gifts, etc.)

_____

_____

_____

17. Did anyone ever take your spouse's/peer's money or did they ever loose money as a child? If yes, how did that make them feel?

_____

_____

_____

18. Did your spouse/peer ever take money from anyone as a child? If yes, how did that make them feel?

_____

_____

_____

Just as learning about yourself in chapter one, learning about your spouse's past or that of your friends and family members is important in understanding your future together. Inside them is a child, a teenager, a twenty-year-old, and so on. An understanding and awareness of others' past experiences opens the opportunity for dialogue and helps to make sure that we're not unconsciously adopting the values and judgments of others regarding money, wealth, and so much more.

Step #7:
Compared to What?

> People seem not to see that their
> opinion of the world is also a
> confession of their character.
> –Ralph Waldo Emerson

Imagine this: you're scheduled to go on vacation for two weeks at some lovely resort or tropical island and you're frantically working to get those longstanding odds and ends tidied up and off your desk before you leave. But just as you're in the middle of breaking through your procrastination, you receive a call. It's your neighbour. There's something wrong at your house and you must go home immediately.

You arrive home, having made your way through a crowd of neighbours and firemen who have gathered in front of your home. You see, with shock and amazement, that your roof has collapsed and a large part of your second floor has crashed into your ground-floor living room. You're beside yourself. How could this have happened? "What a tragedy," you start murmuring to yourself, and then it hits you—"I'm supposed to leave on vacation tomorrow. Oh God, why do these things always happen to me?"

Although a roof collapsing on your home is hardly a tragedy, you can probably relate to an event like this that seems devastating at first but once put into perspective isn't so bad after all. I guess the question is: whose perspective?

So let's back up. Pretend that this incident did happen to you, but make a small change in the story.

You've just returned from the Middle East after reviewing your company's failing division there. You've had guns pointed in your face, faced check-stops where the police shouted at your driver in a foreign language, and have narrowly avoided several car bombings.

A week after your return, you come home to the same

scenario as before. Your roof has collapsed and you realize that you're not going to make your vacation flight the following morning. What's your reaction? Would it be a bit different? After all, you're in a free country, no one has a gun in your face, you've never heard of a car bombing in your city, ever, and you've got house insurance. Not a big deal. After all, no one was hurt, not even Fluffy the cat, because you weren't able to get him back in the house that morning before you left for work.

If that didn't do the trick of putting the incident into perspective, let's take the collapsing roof example one more time, minus the Middle East trip. This time, you get a call on your cell phone from your spouse five minutes after you arrive at your home, which is in shambles. Your child has just been in a major accident and you have no idea how serious the situation is. The house is suddenly the least of your concerns and is not very important at all, is it? It's the same event each time, yet I'm sure you'll agree that it becomes far less significant after a return from a troubling place in the world or when faced with a life-and-death situation of a loved one. It's all about perspective.

In terms of perspective, there's an old saying: Wherever you go, there you are. I have, as wonderful friends, two couples who, coincidentally, both moved from their respective cities one weekend and each called me one Sunday evening to let me know how the move had gone.

The first couple I spoke with had moved from Calgary to Edmonton. The wife told me she couldn't wait to get out of Calgary. The city had become too big, too fast and people were always in a hurry, rude, and too pushy for her liking. So, after living for over twenty years in Calgary, she had left for the seemingly quieter location of Edmonton.

The husband of the second couple I spoke with told me of a huge and unexpected snowstorm that had blown into Calgary that Sunday morning. This couple had moved to Calgary from Vancouver and he reported that he was overwhelmed and shocked by the friendliness and courtesies extended to them by his new home city, Calgary. He also commented on how slow-paced the city seemed. To this day, he loves every minute in his new city.

How could the first couple have such a different take on the same city? How could Calgary be warm and friendly to one couple and cold and fast-paced to another? Perspective makes all the difference. And, by the way, the couple who moved from Calgary to Edmonton now find, just two short years later, that their new home city is just as cold and unfriendly as their last. Could they, and not their surroundings, be the main contributing factor that leads to their opinion of each city?

Embrace Your Critics

The mediocre mind is incapable of understanding the man who refuses to bow blindly to conventional prejudices and chooses instead to express his opinions courageously and honestly.
–Albert Einstein

It seems that nothing is ever good enough for the critics. As I pondered this subject more, I thought about chefs and restaurateurs and how absurd it would be for them to serve only one item on their menu. There's a reason a restaurant's menu usually lists over a dozen items. Not everyone wants or likes the same thing. Can you imagine a situation where a chef puts on an event for hundreds of individuals, is told to serve the same dish to all of these people only to become upset if some of the guests complain or criticize the meal? Well, we'd probably tell the chef not to worry about it because it's almost impossible to custom cater to the needs of hundreds of different palates. So why, then, are we upset when we start on the journey of our dreams and encounter opposition or criticism?

Marilyn vos Savant, one of the most brilliant women of our time, is listed in the *Guinness Book of World Records* as having the highest recorded IQ in history. She has an interesting take on critics in her book *Ask Marilyn*. She points to the invention of the light bulb. Although significant and a truly life-changing invention, the light bulb still has its limitations. It can light a room, but it won't light your entire house. It's also very fragile and will break if dropped. She sums up the critic thus:

> ...the critic remains silent in the darkness, but curses the light bulb as soon as somebody invents it. In science, those who can, do; those who can't, criticize.

After all, what's easier? Building an office tower or burning it down?

As you focus your energies on your goals and dreams, you might find that the more you focus and the more imminent success becomes, the more likely you are to face criticism. You can't please everyone. Most of us know this at a logical level yet we take it personally when a negative comment comes our way.

At the same time as you learn to free yourself from the opinions of your critics, I encourage you to embrace your critics even though this might seem to be paradoxical. Critics can also be teachers. Although we love nothing more than to receive praise and encouragement for everything we do, critics can offer clues for improvements that we have overlooked.

I remember hearing at a young age a quote that I have held near to my heart ever since: "Living well is the best revenge." We often would enjoy taking our revenge on those who have criticized us in the past, but to live well is truly to embrace the critics in our lives and to use their sometimes cruel assessments to our own advantage.

> Any fool can criticize, condemn,
> and complain—and most fools do.
> –Dale Carnegie

I remember a criticism I received from a boyfriend of mine in my very early adulthood that has shaped my life ever since. This fellow was a very successful businessman but when he didn't know something, he would pretend he did. At the time, I had two job opportunities of a lifetime presented to me. The yearly salary was about $50,000 for one position and the other was offering around $32,000. Even the lower amount was impressive and exciting as I was barely twenty at the time, but when I sought the counsel of my boyfriend and his business acumen to help me make a decision between the two, his comments shocked me to my core. He said swiftly and confidently, "Don't be silly, you'll be lucky if you ever earn $50,000 in your entire life." You can imagine how shocked I was at his lack of belief in my abilities and talents.

At the end of the day, I did settle on the job with the lower salary because the other company pulled its offer at the last minute, citing corporate cutbacks, but the story has a great ending.

I kept in touch with the person doing the hiring for the company that pulled back and was offered another job within six months. I worked happily for that company for many successful years. The best news of all was that I used my past boyfriend's criticism to live well and prove him wrong. I used his stinging words to hone my skills and achieve what he (and I) had never thought possible. I'm also happy to report that, by my mid-twenties, I was earning more than he was and much more than he had estimated I could earn in a lifetime. That's called living well!

Summary

- Schedule worry. If you're going to engage in this useless thought process, at least limit your exposure and do it productively and intelligently.
- Go big or go home. Learn to experience your emotions fully, but put a time limit on them.
- Feel the fear and do it anyway, and remember that fear is a natural part of life.

- Focus on what you want and more of it will show up in your life.
- Remember what you've previously overcome, and it will serve you in handling your task at hand.
- Come from a spirit of gratitude, appreciation, and love. If you can only think one thought at any given time, why not choose these?
- Develop a positive support group and learn how others have solved the problem you might be facing.
- Compared to what? Put your problems into perspective.
- Embrace your critics. They could have valuable lessons disguised as criticism. Remember, crows only pick at the best fruit, so know when to disregard a negative comment.

Your Prosperity Action Steps

- Change your current environment with simple steps. Replace a regular fluorescent bulb with a full spectrum one, listen to relaxing music to block out background noise, and try an uplifting essential-oil diffuser to enhance the air that you take in daily.
- If you have regular Monday to Friday workweeks, Sunday evening is a great time to schedule an appointment with yourself. Since most workers dread Monday morning, why not shut the television off on Sunday evening and plan all of the activities that you would like to focus on for the days ahead. What issues or problems are imminent in the coming week? Grab a fresh sheet of paper or a new page in your journal and work through each issue consciously. Perhaps you should book a coffee date or call a friend or professional and have them support you in solving your dilemma.
- Equally as effective on a Sunday evening is a recap session. List all of the negative and ineffective emotions that you experienced the previous week. How

long did you indulge in each of them? Set a time period for normal negative emotions, such as only 30 minutes for anger, 15 minutes for frustration, and so on.

• What are you fearful of accomplishing? What steps can you take to overcome or work with your fear? Tackle one fearful challenge this week and find at least ten solutions for overcoming it. Choose the best one and take action!

Chapter Seven
You, Inc.

Work is love made visible.
–Kahlil Gibran

Determining "You, Inc."

Statistics show that you're likely to change your career path a number of times in your working lifetime. A study was published examining the number of times baby boomers (those born between 1957 to 1964) changed jobs between the ages eighteen and thirty-six. Shockingly, the boomers held and average of 9.6 jobs in this short span of their life. (Source: The Bureau of Labor Statistics. August 2002, "Number of Jobs Held, Labor Market Activity, and Earnings Growth among Younger Baby Boomers: Results from More Than Two Decades of Longitudinal Survey.") According to James C. Cabera and Charles Albrecht Jr., authors of *The Lifetime Career Manager*, in today's employment environment, most Canadians change careers at least once and change companies at least four times.

Assuming that even though you might not make as many career or job changes as the average boomer, you're still likely to make a few in your lifetime. You're also statistically likely to not enjoy your job at all, and possibly the stress or lack of inspiration could affect your health. Well, if you're not doing what you absolutely love, then why not?

As we examined in some of the previous chapters, it's essential to know where we stand when it comes to our job satisfaction. If we're ever going to find that ideal position that fills our life with excitement and fulfillment, we first need to analyze our current employment status.

Self-Assessment Questionnaire #3
Rating Your Employment Satisfaction Level

1. Do you currently enjoy your job? Explain.

_____

_____

_____

2. Do you enjoy the field that you work in? Explain.

_____

_____

_____

3. What do you enjoy the most about your current position?

_____

_____

_____

4. What do you enjoy the least about your current position?

_____

_____

_____

5. Would you like to work fewer hours? Why or why not?

_____

_____

_____

6. Would you like to work more hours? Why or why not?

_____

_____

_____

7. Are you being fully challenged? Explain.

_____

_____

_____

8. Are you being paid fairly? Are you being paid to your full potential?

_____

_____

_____

9. What would be your ideal compensation? What would it consist of (salary, bonuses, other perks)?

_____

_____

_____

10. What first attracted to you to your job?

_____

_____

_____

11. What first attracted to you to the field that you work in?

_____

_____

_____

12. Have they changed? Have you changed? Explain.

_____

_____

_____

If your primary career consists of staying at home with your children or taking care of your home, or both, please fill out the above questionnaire anyway. The job or field doesn't matter; what's important is that no job has to be a life sentence. You have the freedom and flexibility to entertain employment options that you've actively considered.

Getting fired is nature's way to telling you
that you had the wrong job in the first place.
–Hal Lancaster

If you've never attended a workshop or read a book on selecting the ideal career, it's essential that you take a few moments to determine what's really important to you. In chapter six, we identified that when we set goals, we sometimes don't look at them in their entirety and holistically in contrast to the other goals in our life. The same is true when we think a job or field is ideal only to later be disappointed with some aspect that we hadn't fully considered beforehand. Take a few moments to daydream about your ideal job and what that means to you specifically, even if you're not considering a career change at the moment.

Determining Your Ideal Job

1. What time of day would you like to go to work?

_____

2. How many hours in a day would you like to work?

_____

3. How many days per week would you like to work?

_____

4. Where would you like work? (i.e. at home, in an office, in a huge office tower, etc.)

_____

5. How would you get to work? (i.e. as a passenger, as a driver, taking the public transportation system.)

_____

6. At home or another workplace, what would your ideal office be like? Would you have an office?

_____

7. Would you have a boss or would you be the boss?

_____

8. Would you have employees or an assistant?

_____

9. Would you like new challenges from your work? Explain.

_____

_____

_____

10. Would you like less stress from your work? Explain.

_____

_____

_____

11. Would you like flexibility or consistency in your schedule?

_____

_____

_____

12. Would you like flexibility or consistency in your income?

_____

_____

_____

13. Would you like benefits and bonuses?

_____

14. Would you like more responsibility or less? Explain.

_____

_____

_____

15. How would you like to be acknowledged at work (more pay, advancement, etc.)?

_____

_____

_____

I was surprised to learn from a 2005 Ipsos-Reid survey for RBC Financial Group that about 3.2 million adult Canadians, or 13.5%, said that they would like to start their own businesses. Roughly 950,000 of them hope to do so within one year.

I believe that the entrepreneurial spirit is more alive today than ever in history. As a business owner myself, I've had several people express their interest in owning their own business. I would always have these individuals complete the above questionnaire for consistency and likelihood of success.

Let's say, for example, that you completed the above questionnaire and would like to open your own business. You've identified that you'd like the flexibility and freedom that comes with being an entrepreneur, would like maximum challenge, and don't mind the extra stress that comes with starting a new business. But let's assume that you desire a regular paycheque and cannot handle variances in your salary. Let's also assume that you have children and definitely cannot afford to put in evenings or weekends. If you had answered this way and had come to me for advice on opening a financial planning firm, I would carefully caution you to do otherwise. So often the allure of owning a business, with its freedom and absolute control, is overshadowed by the long hours, grunt work, and lack of certainty or security regarding income or time spent at work.

It would be just as defeating for someone who is interested in unlimited flexibility, pay, and advancement to take a position such as a teacher. We know that the education field usually requires a regular schedule and has fairly set salaries without bonuses or commissions. There are, however, exceptions to every rule. Nevertheless, why create more obstacles for yourself at the outset than necessary?

If you'd like to work in a fancy office tower, wear a suit, and punch a clock, go downtown one day and look at the companies that are listed in the towers' directories. It will give you a good idea as to the type of position that might exist for you if that lifestyle is of interest. Start to interview your friends, family, and associates. Find out what they really do in a day at work. If their job title or field sounds intimidating or unfamiliar, just ask them to describe what they do in a typical day. That should give you an idea as to what that position might encompass. Further investigate by asking such questions as: Who are your customers? Who are your wholesalers? What do you enjoy most/least about your job? What did you do before this job? What education or training was required?

If you completed the above questionnaire and realized how much you really do need a job change, but for whatever reason you cannot or are just not ready for a change, there's great news for you too! Think about all of the activities that you're good at, enjoy, or love and figure out a way to capitalize on them. They could be hobbies or skills that come particularly easy to you that you could try turning into a side business for fun.

Assuming that you love filing taxes and enjoy working with numbers, why not take a tax-filing course and offer to file the returns of your friends and family members for a discounted rate? If you love painting or are a consummate artist, why not take a course on creating your own web site and market your wares world wide and on your free time. Better yet, teach a beginners how-to course on your craft.

> Nothing is really work unless you would
> rather be doing something else.
> –James M. Barrie

If you don't have any hobbies or interests that you feel could generate a side income, try volunteering. Early in my career, though it was never a goal of mine to enter the financial industry, I found that I missed the excitement of the marketing and communications training that I studied in college. I did have some opportunities in my career to market the overall firm but not to the level I would have liked. Understanding that I had no real experience in advertising and marketing, I would likely be turned down if I applied for such a position. But they were my corporate passion and forte, so I decided to apply and expand my skills on a volunteer basis.

I volunteered for a number of committees and within a year, I was chairing a committee and soon served on a few boards. During my volunteering years, I learned what school and my current jobs could never have taught me. I networked with city councillors and the mayor and countless other prominent business people in my city at only twenty years old. Wearing the hat of a volunteer position can open many wonderful opportunities that could easily lead you on the path to a new job or career.

Developing "You, Inc."

Why do companies expend all of the resources, time, and energy they do to design policies? It's because they know that advanced thinking formed into structured procedures equals success—if implemented and monitored. And when these policies are examined and improved, a company's employees will have a successful plan to follow.

It's been said that rules are like pie shells, they're meant to be broken, but if you don't know what your rules are, how will you know when you've broken them?

If you were an employee, why would you care about thinking of yourself as a personal corporation? First, there's the strange phenomenon that I've experienced in my short twelve-year professional career. It's the experience of bumping into someone you knew from school, past jobs, or other areas of your life; somehow, you cross that person's path again in an unexpected way. No matter what size your city is, you've likely experienced this "it's a small world after all" situation. It sometimes comes out of Murphy's Law, doesn't it? That person you've just flipped the bird to in traffic might be attending the job interview or client meeting that you're scheduled for later in the day.

What are your rules for life and when do you break them? Do you even know if you've broken them? If rules are meant to be broken, shouldn't you at least know when you've broken your own? Do you think some much-needed clarity could come into your life if you actually knew what *your* rules are, if you had a corporate policy statement that is flexible enough for the corporation of You, Inc.? And when do you break your rules? Do you have a different set of rules for business conduct than for your personal life?

Love him or hate him, we all remember the moral debates in coffee shops and around water coolers on the subject of former U.S. President Bill Clinton. Many conversations I overheard went something like this: "Yeah, maybe he is a dog in his personal life, cheating on his wife all those times and then being caught in sexual misconduct with his intern, *but he was a great president.* He fixed the economy, helped the environment, and his personal life should be his personal life."

What do you think? Have you ever bent the rules because they didn't apply personally or within your work situation? Would you consider yourself to be an honest citizen who would never cheat or steal yet you find some way to justify fighting a speeding ticket that you know darn well you deserved? And having discovered, after arriving home from a long night of Christmas shopping, that the sales clerk didn't charge you for a $50 purchase, would you convince yourself that they'll never miss it because they're such a big store anyway? Do you even give any of these issues any thought at all?

I was blessed enough when I entered the financial industry to have a boss who was willing to take me under his wing, who truly had a heart of gold, and who led a life of impeccability. I knew he was respected in his industry but it wasn't until I left his financial planning firm that I truly understood the importance of living by your own personal policies and knowing when you've broken them.

My boss had a quote that he truly lived by and would

often say out loud during our meetings or when making difficult decisions: "Act as if the entire world is watching, especially when no one is watching." He would go so far as to call another financial advisor whose client wanted to join our firm.

Whenever I have mentioned to colleagues in the industry that my first apprenticeship was with Wayne, the response is always: "Wow, you were lucky to have worked with such a great man." This is what his competitors were saying. Can you imagine what his friends and family say about him? He knew somehow that even if *no one* is watching, it all counts because *someone* is watching—you. And each time you commit a personal "crime," no matter how big or small, it has a significant impact on that tiny voice inside your head that says you're a great person, you're worthy, you are a person of your word. You deserve to hold yourself in high esteem. Each simple and small act works towards building your self-esteem at many levels, even though "no one" is watching.

Holding Yourself to a Higher Standard

> It is not how much we do,
> but how much love we put into the doing.
> –Mother Teresa

So now that you're the *president* and not just some employee who follows someone else's rules, *you* make the rules! What's your stance like? How do you dress for work? What goals and dreams are you making happen? What's your plan?

After creating a great plan that includes clear and defined policies for their employees to follow, many companies make the mistake of allowing it to sit in some drawer or cabinet and never look at it again. This should be a work in progress. It might take you six months to a year to discover many of the rules you need to move on to the next stage of making your personal policy statement. Start today! On a fresh pad of paper, begin to jot down your observations about your own behaviour and that of others. This will begin the process of creating rules that will allow you to live a freer and more effortless life.

How do you start such a seemingly daunting and obscure task? Begin by noticing your upsets. Each time you're upset with something you've done or something someone else has done or failed to do, you've broken one of your personal rules. It might be obvious or it might take a little digging, but with each upset, you'll discover a new ideal to live by in the future. It's been said that a mid-life crisis occurs when individuals decide that they're now going to live by their own rules. After a lifetime of being told by parents, teachers, employers, and others how to live and what to think, and having decisions forced upon them, the light bulb goes on.

Now, you might be thinking that more rules are the last thing you need in your life because you have enough to follow already. I agree. You probably have many rules imposed on you on a daily basis, but these are going to be *your* rules, and with these clear rules and your personal policies, I guarantee that freedom will follow.

Your Personal Inventory

I'd bet that you know more about your liabilities than your assets. And I'd also bet that you're really good at pointing out your failures and shortcomings, and, if this is the case, you could be in deep trouble. If your financial balance sheet is out of alignment and your net worth is negative, you need to look at where you want to go and what's going to get you there. Yes, there's merit in understanding and doing some analysis of what went wrong so that you can learn from your mistakes; just don't live in them!

Create a balance sheet of your personal assets. Think of everything you're good at and write it down. You don't need to worry about how you can turn your strengths into profit, just list all of them. Are you a great listener, parent, personal coach? Do you have a university degree, specialized training, or a wonderful understanding of English or a second language? Are you a master in the kitchen, a superb interior designer? The secret to success certainly starts with understanding your skills and assets. I also encourage you to list a few of your liabilities as well; just ensure that you take the time to detail the solutions and action steps needed to overcome them.

Take a moment now to list your top five or ten assets, and over time add to this list as you realize what you're quite skilled at and where your strengths lie.

1. _____
2. _____
3. _____
4. _____
5. _____

Whenever I've sat down with clients and had them fill out a net-worth statement, no matter how wealthy or how far away from monetary wealth they were, they've always found that they had more than originally thought. The fear of looking at what we have and the doubts of whether we'll be in a positive position once the list is complete are completely unfounded. We tend to have more than we at first assume and it all starts with realizing what we do have. Try it; I know you'll be surprised at your personal inventory too!

Personal Policies

> This above all:
> to thine own self be true.
> –William Shakespeare

How do you view your employer? As an employer or as a client who is buying services from You, Inc.? Do you treat your employer as a client who is supporting your company or do you show up 5 minutes late and leave 10 minutes early? Did you know that just 15 minutes per day of downtime at work adds up to over 10 days of downtime per year? Your employer might pay for this time but *life* will *not*!

If the company you worked for were a ship and it was sinking, the priority of the ship's captain (your boss) would be to save the ship. The captain would get rid of all unnecessary cargo to lighten the load until smooth sailing was once again achieved. Only what is absolutely necessary would be kept. Are you valuable and necessary cargo at your place of employment? Are you a vital crew member on your employer's ship or are you just "showing up" or putting in time? If pink slips were handed out tomorrow at your workplace, would your name be anywhere near the top of the list?

> It's not enough to be busy,
> so are the ants. The question is,
> what are we busy about?
> –Henry David Thoreau

Now let's flip the situation around. What if you worked the 15 minutes per day that most people waste? So now you're showing up on time and maybe even leaving 10 minutes later than everybody else. Now you might be saying: "Hey, I already work hard enough for my boss, with low pay and little to no recognition for the contribution I'm making. Why would I want to give my boss one minute more than I'm being paid for?" This thought is why it's vitally important to think of yourself as a company.

If you took on only one major client (your employer) and from time to time—or even at the start of your contract with your new client—you sometimes put in more work than you were paid for, many would assure you that such efforts are required and should be thought of as paying your "dues," just as the owner of any start-up company must do. You would want to create a name for yourself and your company and build your reputation in the community. You would be certain that when the demand for your company's product or service had risen, your profits would increase accordingly.

This new thought process works regardless of whether you're a server at a restaurant or a vice-president of a national corporation. Treat your employer (or prospective employer, if you're now looking for work) as a client of You, Inc. and you will experience amazing and profound effects in your life.

> You cannot kill time
> without injuring eternity.
> –Henry David Thoreau

What if you despise your job? Have you already started looking for another job because you can't stand each moment that you spend in your present job? Have you at least thought about it? Well, first off, you have some major decisions to make. Why are you still there? How long will you allow yourself to live like this? Now, if you're thinking about using those 15 minutes per day to look for a new job on the boss's dime, you might want to think again. The reputation of You, Inc. is on the line and if you are going out, then go out with a *positive* bang!

If you were your boss, what would you think about an employee who spends office time looking for a new job or idly chatting with friends via e-mail? Maybe this is why you don't enjoy your job, you aren't paid what you think you are worth, and you aren't receiving the recognition you deserve.

What if you spent that time doing that little extra that makes all the difference? How about doing some extra filing for the entire office? (Especially if that isn't *your* job—remember, you're pleasing a client.) Why not make a couple of extra calls a day, e-mail the boss with a new idea or an alert about what the competition is up to, or just make your shop a spotless place of business? What type of valuable cargo would you be then if rough seas should arise?

And if for some reason these new efforts go unnoticed at first, don't be concerned, life will eventually notice them. Furthermore, this is the new level of excellence that you've committed to, whether someone is taking note or not. Your goal should be to *wow* your boss regardless of whether this is your last week on the job or part of your journey to a ten-year position. If you owned the company that you now work for and you knew what type of employee you are, would you keep *you* on?

> Paying attention to simple little things that
> most men neglect makes a few men rich.
> –Henry Ford

The Customer Comes Second

Are you a person who over-promises and under-delivers? Why do you do it? Do you find yourself trying to please everyone and ending up displeasing yourself the most? As the most important person in your corporation, you now have a duty—a duty to look after yourself for the sake of the overall viability of your corporation.

A couple of years ago, I was at a corporate conference and was lucky enough to hear a talk given by one of the executives of WestJet. His stories were fascinating and the one that resonated with me the most was that they *never* put their customers first. I was shocked by this statement. What did he mean they didn't put their customers first? From the beginning of sales school, we are taught that the customer always comes first.

WestJet's story is a little different. The *employee* always comes first and the customer second. The reasoning for this unusual policy is that it's easier to find a new customer than it is to find a new employee.

I found this to be one of the most profound business statements of my career. Of course, we've had it backwards all along. Companies spend millions of dollars on hiring, training, and finding ways to keep their employees happy and to profit the overall corporation. If that employee is made to feel in the wrong for the sake of one customer, the company loses so much more in the long run. In addition to potentially losing all of its investment in that employee's training and education, it also weakens employee morale and leaves the impression of an uncaring company.

As the sole employee of You, Inc., how often are you sacrificing your corporate self-esteem for the customer? If you're a salaried employee of one company, you have one major customer. Is that customer worthy of you? If you're a business owner, figure out the "wince factor" of each of your customers or clients.

The wince factor is simple: each time you see that customer or hear the person's name on your voicemail or see it on the screen display, do you wince at the very thought? Perhaps it's time to pass that client on to someone who can relate better to that individual and so free you up to meet with the customers you truly love. But what if this client represents a large account for your firm? Certainly, the importance of the customer and the size of the customer's account make this decision more difficult, but imagine a work environment that you love and that loves you.

I'm not suggesting that every time you have an issue with a client, you immediately try to cull the account or pass it off to someone else, but I am suggesting that you look at those customers who simply drain your energy and imagine what it might be like to deal with only your best customers. After all, with all of the energy you're spending on the wincers, you might have little left over for those who truly deserve your time. And if you're a salaried employee and your largest and only account happens to be your employer, perhaps now is the time to entertain a new employer.

Creating Your Personal Policies

> It takes less time to do things right
> than to explain why you did it wrong.
> –Henry Wadsworth Longfellow

Here are some useful questions to ask yourself in order to determine the rules that work best for you:

What do you wear when you're working?

Whether you work at home or in an office, it's important to establish a work uniform. This might seem like a simple notion, but a corporate uniform will allow you to mentally focus when wearing it and to relax when you take it off. In my field, the rules are fairly blurred on acceptable work attire. There's quite a mix between suits and sweaters, with the latter chosen by those who do not wear a formal suit. I remember a lesson that answered this question for me very early in my career.

I was running my first trade show. It was in a suburb of Edmonton and the attendees were mostly farmers. I thought it would be appropriate to dress more casually and wear a sweater and casual slacks because it was winter and the attendees would mostly be wearing jeans. I was overwhelmed with comments such as, "Oh, you city people can't even dress up for us farmers!"

I was shocked at their attitudes and since it was a two-day trade show, I arrived the next day in a suit. I had obviously read my crowd all wrong. Again, I was shocked at the comments. "Oh yeah, you city people in your suits, thinking that you're too good for us farmers." I couldn't believe it. There was no pleasing these people, but the truth is *there's no pleasing everyone*, so why not start with pleasing yourself?

Then and there I decided that a suit was my personal and ideal work uniform and, for the last decade or so, I've always worn, at the very least, a jacket or formal suit during my work hours. Even on the few occasions in my career that I have worked from home and wasn't to leave the house for any client appointments, I always put on a suit during my workday. What's your ideal work uniform?

When do you handle the most challenging task of the day?

Do you wait until the last hour of your day, fretting about it for hours? Handle the most difficult task of your day first thing in the morning and you'll find power and strength in doing so.

How are you going to get everything done?

Write down the six things that you need to accomplish each day. Start the night before or first thing that morning and write down only six. Then, list them in order of importance and keep that paper with you all day. Start with the first on your list and stay with that task until it's completed or for as long as is possible. Then go on to the next, and so on.

If you can't get your list completed in a day, you wouldn't have been able to do it anyway. By writing down only six tasks, you greatly reduce the chances of feeling overwhelmed or that you have a hundred things to do in a day. Once your list of six is complete, you can go on to the next. I encourage you to keep a separate log of secondary to-do's and if while focusing on your primary list you think of other tasks that are important, write them on your secondary list. This way, you will keep focused on the tasks at hand and will know that when they're done, you will have not missed any details. You will handle the rest later.

Do you play the sex card?

Whether it's a style of dress or innocent flirtation, when it comes to work, there's no room for sex. Playing the sex card reduces the validity of your talents. As a strong woman who knows what she's good at, why imply that it's only your femininity that got you to where you are?

How's your timing?

Do you arrive early for work and appointments and allow for traffic and weather-related delays, or are you the type of person who is always late, who rushes out the door desperately in need of a cup of coffee at work before you become human in the morning? If you were to arrive 15 minutes before any appointment, you would be able to relax and focus your efforts so that you could enter your meetings calmly and poised. If you work for one employer, remember that this is your client. Waking up a few minutes earlier will ensure that you make a great impression each and every morning on your employer and co-workers.

What are your rules regarding social interaction at work?

Is it okay for you to consume alcohol or drink to excess at the staff Christmas party? Do you agree with dating on the job? How about letting loose with clients or co-workers?

The great thing about thinking of yourself as a corporation is that *you* make the rules. Although at times the questions above might seem unnecessary, and possibly you won't always follow your own rules, it is important to know when you've broken a rule that you have set for yourself. And how will you know if you've broken one of your own policies if you've never taken the time to identify that policy?

> Work like you don't need the money.
> –Mark Twain

Wherever you find yourself in life, *you* made the appointment to be there. All of the choices you made in the past have led you to where you are right now. The great thing about realizing this, whether you like where you are or not, is that you have the power to change your situation by changing the little steps that move you in the direction of your desires. Do you wish you had a different relationship from the one you currently have? Then what are you doing now to change it? In five years, what will your relationship look like? The same as it does now, but with more bitterness and resentment, or will it be filled with passion and love because of the steps for change that you identified?

You have *absolute* control over where you are and where you're going because if you don't have control over you, who does? Is there a higher outside power over your life? Absolutely! What's the mix—50/50, 60/40? We'll never know. But so often in our lives, we're not happy with something we create. We make the choices and blame God or the universe. We ask why this has happened to us. It happens to everyone. Generally speaking, you have the ability to change your surroundings. There are people who had a lot less and did a lot more!

Words Have Power

The words we speak have great power, as do the words we think. In chapter two, we identified that some words and phrases referring to money, such as "filthy rich" and "too rich for my blood," have power. Do you know that it's been said that people who use the phrase "[So-and-so] is a pain in the ass" are much more likely to develop hemorrhoids? While that's somewhat amusing, and whether or not it's an old wives' tale, when we say a word, we are sending a command to our nervous system and are focusing on that word, even if we think it has no bearing on our life.

How many positive words do you have to describe a wonderful experience? When was the last time you felt *elated* or filled with *bliss*? Do these words exist in your vocabulary? Take a moment to write down five positive words. If you need to find a thesaurus or go on the Internet to look for some, do that now. I would suggest you check out www.dictionary.com because this site has a wonderful thesaurus feature. Just type in "happy" or "fantastic" or any of the usual words you use to describe your positive experiences, then write down some alternatives.

1. _____
2. _____
3. _____
4. _____
5. _____

Over the next few weeks, try to use these words in addition to your regular vocabulary and see what happens. See if your experience changes as you use new words to describe that experience. The same principle works with your self-talk.

What about our negative experiences? I would guess that you can easily think up many more words to describe your less positive life events. When was the last time you were angry, frustrated, enraged, depressed, blue, and on and on?

I have a wonderful friend who often feels frustrated. He uses this word to describe his reactions to his day, his work, his family, and sometimes his friends. And how does he generally feel? Frustrated, of course. He tried the simple exercise of changing this frequently used word in his vocabulary and it changed his life. He decided to use the term "mildly miffed" in place of "frustrated." When he told me about the challenges of his day after using his new word, he would actually smile and laugh a little as he described some very challenging events. This new lightness came from just changing his use of words.

When you ask someone how they're doing, how often will the person sigh and proclaim, "Busy, very, very busy." Everyone is so "busy" these days, and as a society, we put great emphasis on this word. In the corporate arena, we might want the other person to know how busy we are to gain a spark of empathy or because we don't want more work piled on our desk. But at the end of the day, this simple word, which many of us use to describe our entire day, causes us to go home feeling tired and exhausted from being so busy.

A very good friend of mine pointed out a new phrase to me last year and I've been using it whenever the opportunity arises. These words have totally revolutionized how I think about my workday. He suggested trying the phrase, "Well, it's a bit crazier than I'd like—but I'm still having fun."

I took his advice and the first couple of people I said this to must have been very incredulous because at the time I wasn't just a "little bit busy"—I was frantic and swamped, and I wasn't having any fun at all. But after a while, and I couldn't believe how many times in a day I had the opportunity to use my new phrase, I was able to put my day into perspective. My friend had given me a gift of focus with my new words, and within a few weeks, I found congruency each time I stated this new phrase. I was actually having fun! Just a simple re-framing and a few new words changed my entire experience and, at the end of the day, put those inquiring after me at ease as well. After all, who wants to continue a conversation with someone who feels busy, swamped, or frantic?

Also, at a very early age, I chose to completely delete a popular word from my vocabulary, and this has too revolutionized my life. I grew up observing a family member who was often severely depressed. I watched this person suffer many years of this illness and, though still young, thought at a very early age, "Well, what if I don't believe in the option of being in a depressed mood and never use the word *depression*?" The result? The word *depression* truly doesn't exist for me. I understand that it is a word that many use to describe their feelings but it wasn't one I would ever use. As a result, I can happily and wholeheartedly report that I have *never* been in a depressed mood. I've been sad, blue, worried, and experienced a few other less-than-wonderful states, but *never* depressed; it's not even an option.

Ponder the following words of Ella Wheeler Wilcox, who so eloquently expresses the importance of a positive self attitude for attracting more of what you would like in your life. I would add that both your thoughts and your spoken words manifest an ideal attitude and life.

Solitude

Laugh, and the world laughs with you;
Weep, and you weep alone,
For the sad old earth must borrow its mirth,
But has trouble enough of its own.
Sing, and the hills will answer;
Sigh, it is lost on the air,
The echoes bound to a joyful sound,
But shrink from voicing care.

Rejoice, and men will seek you;
Grieve, and they turn and go.
They want full measure of all your pleasure,
But they do not need your woe.
Be glad, and your friends are many;
Be sad, and you lose them all,—
There are none to decline your nectar'd wine,
But alone you must drink life's gall.

Feast, and your halls are crowded
Fast, and the world goes by.
Succeed and give, and it helps you live,
But no man can help you die.
There is room in the halls of pleasure
For a long and lordly train,
But one by one we must all file on
Through the narrow aisles of pain.

Ella Wheeler Wilcox

Try this simple technique. Write down five words you currently use that are not serving you any longer.

1. _____
2. _____
3. _____

4. _____

5. _____

Now, pull that thesaurus back out or pop back on the Internet, and find five new words or phrases that would better focus your mind or soften the impact of the word you're currently using.

If you find that there are times when your old word would more appropriately describe your experience and a substitute doesn't work or you just need to wallow a bit in some mood, go ahead. Just re-read the section entitled "Go Big or Go Home" in chapter six and make sure that you put a time limit on your negative feelings and thoughts. Be sure to give yourself ample time to feel what occurs in your life—anger, sadness, worry—but don't allow these feelings to consume you. Schedule them when possible, feel their intensity, and set an alarm clock to alert you to when it's time to focus on being more constructive.

> Sometimes I've believed as many as six
> impossible things before breakfast.
> –Lewis Carroll, *Alice in Wonderland*

The Dangers of Universals

When was the last time someone told you that you never do something right or you always do some other thing wrong? A universal is a word that someone uses to make a statement to you that makes a sweeping judgment, whether intentional or unintentional.

Universals are dangerous because they don't factor in any reasonable exception. You might tell your spouse, "You never take the garbage out," when this statement is perhaps only true this week. Your boss might tell you that you're always late when it might only be the second time you've been late in months. Have you ever caught yourself using a universal when judging yourself? Have you ever accused yourself of "always" making stupid mistakes or never picking the right lover to be with? Universals can make us and others feel hopeless.

Handling Inner and Outer Critics

> To avoid criticism do nothing,
> say nothing, be nothing.
> –Elbert Hubbard

Handling outer critics can be simple and effortless with this easy exercise. Generally, when someone criticizes us, they'll use a universal word or statement. For example, your boss might say, "You're always messing up." You could simply feed this universal back to your boss. "Really boss, I'm *always* messing up?" And what's your boss most likely to say? "Well, I guess you're not *always* messing up." Then, you must follow up with another extremely important question: "How, specifically?" It's one of the most powerful little questions I've ever learned and used in my life.

When we're extremely frustrated or feeling overwhelmed, one act can often seem like the total sum of a person. You're *always* messing up—whatever you did specifically to receive the castigation of your boss, might have felt to her, even if it was one episode, that you really were *always* messing up. And if we use what we learned in chapter three, that what we focus on expands but that we can only focus on so many bits of information, a redirect can have staggering results. If you were to ask your boss what she specifically means by your messing up, she might say something like, "Well, you botched that sales meeting we had last week and we might lose the client."

First, she's still talking to you and you haven't been fired, so this is a good thing. Second, she's focused on one specific thing now, not waving a blanket of judgment over your entire career performance. You can now ask more empowering and unambiguous questions of your boss such as, "What can we do in the future to ensure that I handle such a meeting to your satisfaction?" Your boss might realize that you need more training or that you have been under a lot of stress and could use a vacation or an assistant. Whatever the result, you want to stop the sweeping generalization of the statement. This simple shift also works wonderfully with yourself, your family, and friends.

Let's say you arrive home late from work and your spouse greets you at the door (you not realizing pizza has been ordered two hours ago and is now cold) and says, "You're always late; you never think of my needs." Again, repeat the statement back, "Really, honey, I'm *always* late and I *never* think of your needs?" You might gently remind your spouse that you called three times last week before arriving home late from the office. This is a great opportunity to set your rules out as a couple and what's expected when coming home later than usual.

Sometimes when a criticism or an exaggerated judgment is cast, a universal doesn't exist. For example, someone might pick up this book and report to me, "Your book is stupid." How does one handle a response like that, assuming I even care to respond? If I did care to inquire further, I might say, "I understand that *you feel* that my book is stupid, but I'm curious, which part of my book did you find beneficial?" Again, I'm feeding back a question that focuses their mind on a more positive note.

No matter who they are, I highly doubt that they didn't learn at least one new thing that could benefit their life in some great way. Do you remember when I asked you not to think of the colour blue? If someone tells me that my book is stupid (and thankfully no one has), I could simply focus their mind on green or red—which part did you enjoy? Which part of my book did you find compelling, inspirational, or enlightening? The likelihood is that their mind will find something positive or constructive to report back to me about.

What about those insidious inner critics—you know the ones. It's your own voice and your own self-talk. Most of us talk to ourselves in negative tones and use disparaging words that we would never tolerate from others but it's somehow acceptable in the solidarity of our minds. When was the last time that you blew a speech, yelled at your child, or did something that deserved self-reproach? Perhaps it sounded something like, "You'll just never get it right. You're a terrible speaker."

I've been a speaker for over a decade now and I can assure you that there are times when I nail a speech and other times when I do not connect with my group for whatever reason, but usually it's somewhere in between. When my critical inner voice is there to meet me after a talk that was less than perfect, it's usually pretty harsh.

The Two Most Powerful Words on Earth

Negative self-talk and self-criticism are inevitable. There are times when you know you could have done better. In the example of giving a talk, perhaps the sound system was acting up or my audience was smaller or larger than anticipated or maybe I just didn't know my material as well as I could have. There are two magical words that Charles Faulkner points out to us in his audio program *Success Mastery with NLP* that can counteract even the toughest of critical voices—the words are "so far."

Get to know these words and if jolting your wrist with the elastic band and focusing on the opposite doesn't work, just add these two words after any critical statement. "I'm a terrible public speaker...so far;" "I just can't sell and will never reach my goals...so far;" I'm an awful mother, spouse, friend, [insert noun here]...so far." By adding these two powerful little words, what does the end of the sentence focus your mind on? For me, it adds hope and encouragement. We're often so focused on being perfect that it is empowering to look at ourselves with some levity. By adding "so far" to a self-defeating thought, you remind yourself that life is a journey and you're a student of life getting better and better every day.

Make Feedback Your Friend

> If I have lost confidence in myself,
> I have the universe against me.
> –Ralph Waldo Emerson

There are no failures in life. We've heard this from some of the greatest minds of our time and of times long past.

In life, feedback is a great friend, and failure our foe. Is this simply semantics? Sure, why not? Each perceived failure in life is actually quite exciting. It's a new road map for the future and if we listen carefully, we'll know what to do better next time, what not to do and so on.

The word *feedback* is also a wonderful way to reframe our focus—just when it's needed. To explain a failure is difficult and can even be humiliating and debilitating. To examine the facts and determine what can improve our lives is empowering and focuses our minds on improving, not dwelling on a past that's unchangeable.

As a public speaker, I can happily report that I've advanced over the years. I had more than my share of bombed talks and have a binder full of areas for improvement. And just like many public speakers, I still get quite nervous before a lecture. But as a seasoned professional, I can usually handle whatever a group or venue throws my way.

I was recently invited to speak at a large woman's show as one of their main stage presenters. This was quite an opportunity for me and an exciting venue indeed. Unfortunately, the stage was set up more for a rock band than a prosperity lecture and the microphone kept feeding back an awful screech. I was somewhat paralyzed on the stage but worked my way through a very painful speech. Being so far away from my audience definitely stunned my normal flow, as did the feedback from the sound system.

Don't be too timid and squeamish
about your actions. All life is an
experiment. The more experiments
you make the better.
–Ralph Waldo Emerson

For a while after this presentation, I was horrified and kept reliving all that had gone wrong. How could I bomb like that with hundreds of presentations under my belt and years of experience? My business coach and a very good friend walked me through the powerful re-frame of failure versus feedback.

First, he awakened me to the fact that I wasn't actually as bad as I thought I was—that the audience actually enjoyed my talk. But since he had attended so many other presentations of mine, he was honest that it certainly wasn't my best job to date. What he had me do there and then was to write down all of what had thrown me off. I listed that I hadn't checked the stage, and I didn't make sure that I had a cordless microphone so I could walk closer to my audience and connect with them, and so on.

Just weeks after that, I had another significant talk booked and was extra nervous because I assumed that I was on a destined path leading to more substandard speeches. I stopped trusting myself for a moment and believed that my last "failure" was going to be the norm from now on. Before this next talk, I took my list of "musts" as a presenter and ensured that the room worked for me and my audience. I used the feedback from my last event and others to focus on a better talk this time around. The result? I'm truly thrilled to report that this talk was my best ever. I was still a little nervous at the start but all of my past "failures" and really taking the feedback to heart as a learned lesson proved effective.

When in Doubt, Act "As If"

Be as you wish to seem.
–Socrates

Socrates and so many others know that sometimes you must act before you actually feel and become what you aspire to be. Do you have a challenge in life, for example, that requires you to be confident when you're scared silly? Try this simple notion: act as if you're a confident person and see what happens.

How would confident people stand? What self-talk would be running through their thoughts? How would they breathe? You might not feel confident as you handle many of your challenges but this game of pretend can produce profound results and, eventually, you might find that you're not pretending at all. What if you have a problem with depression or are in a rut that you can't seem to shake? Well, try on the thought of acting "as if" you are a happy, joyful, and light-hearted person. Would they have a smile on their faces? Perhaps they would sing or whistle a tune. Try this simple exercise in almost any situation where you would like to change how you're feeling. When in doubt, try acting "as if."

Flexibility Equals Opportunity

How many times have you turned on the news or read in the newspaper a story featuring someone that has opened a unique business or come out with a new invention and thought, "I could have done that!" It happens so often. Scotoma is a blind spot that happens to almost everyone and to some of us on a regular basis. How many times have you opened the kitchen cupboard looking for the salt or pepper and maybe even cursed a family member accusing them of moving it? Perhaps over the mumbles and complaining, a family member hears your dilemma and reaches in front of you pulling out the salt shaker with a look of disdain. Humbly, you apologize and swear on your life that it wasn't there just a moment ago.

Scotoma can limit our successes in life too. We often have blind spots and opportunities that, for whatever reason, we just can't see. Creating more flexibility in our daily life will give us the ability, over time, to create a broader view of life and enable us to see what we didn't before.

We often get stuck in the doldrums of life and forget to appreciate the wondrous world around us. When we try or do something new for the first time, it's always exciting. But after a while, even the most exciting experiences and situations become mundane. Think of the first time you saw the love of your life, walked up to your new home or entered your office on the first day of work? Everything was a treat; the smile of your lover, the potential of your new home, and the view in your office. Over the years, we stop noticing the little things and then tread dangerously inside the proverbial "box." As we stop noticing the subtleties of our environment, we limit our possibilities within it, not to mention our ability to enjoy it.

The following are a few fun ideas that were adapted from Charles Faulkner's audio program *Success Mastery with NLP*. They're great for expanding creativity in your life and will work your flexibility muscles.

- Dress differently today. If you usually put on your pants first and then your top, change it up. Put your left sock or nylon on first if you usually aim towards the right.
- Do you usually brush your teeth and then wash your face in the morning? Try the opposite for a week.
- The next time you're driving to or from work, take a different path home; even one block off your normal drive with reveal homes not previously noticed.
- Walk down your street with different eyes, as if for the very first time. Take a stroll around your neigh-

bourhood and really try to notice what you haven't before. Be in the present and take in all of the stimuli around you.

- Be someone else at the grocery store. The next time you're shopping or waiting in line, pretend to be a glamorous movie star, model, or hero of yours. Imagine what it might be like to not want to be noticed and who might be looking your way. Feel, if only for a moment, what it is really like to be that person. Or, perhaps visit a different grocery store the next time you're stocking up. See and interact with the cashiers and other shoppers. Notice how the same chain store is similar but likely laid out differently depending on its location.
- Put yourself in the shoes of someone across from you at a boring meeting. Imagine yourself in their body, what they might be thinking, how they're sitting.

As mentioned previously, children have a natural ability to be in the present and make any event fun and entertaining. Be silly and indulge that still small child within you and look for the wonder in your daily life today and forever. Doing so will clear up your scotoma and unveil exciting new opportunities just waiting to be discovered.

Stop Losses and Checkpoints

If you've ever purchased a stock with a full-service broker, you might know about a practice called a stop loss. When you purchase a stock, you're aware, or quickly made aware, that there are risks associated with your purchase. You hope that it will increase in value but equity market investments are not guaranteed so no matter how sure the bet might seem, there's always the risk of loss. A stop-loss system comes into effect if the stock starts to plummet.

We'll assume that the stock you're going to buy is selling at $20 per share. The conversation with your broker at the start should include your downside exposure. You might tell him that you're hoping the share moves to $25 and at that time he should sell half of it. But should it start to decline, you couldn't handle a loss of more than 25%, for example, so he must start the selling process if the stock should fall to $15.

Would a stop-loss system have helped your investment portfolio in the past? Has your portfolio ever decreased in value by much more than you anticipated or even knew to be possible? Did you realize that you could only handle a 10% drop in your investment values after your portfolio had already tumbled 40%?

Think about how this simple system in the investment world might be effective in your own life. How simple it would be, for example, to identify at the start a "stop loss" in our relationships and careers? Have you ever stayed at a job or a relationship you knew you should have left years before? Did you stay for a 40% loss when you could only handle 10%? Have you let an innocent habit get out of control and take over your life?

I remember a time in my life when sugar cravings took hold of me and my appetite for chocolate bars became insatiable. At an all-time low in my health plan, I was up to five chocolate bars every day. Looking back, I can't understand why I didn't at least govern my bad habit to some degree. How much easier it would have been to move past my sugar cravings if I had imposed limits upon myself. How about two chocolate bars a day or even three?

But I just kept sailing higher until finally one day I had had enough. How did I know that five was the magic chocolate bar number, the number that was to determine my limit? Why not ten per day or more? Somewhere within my subconscious, I had determined five to be the magic number. Why not do this process consciously?

We all have bad habits we wish we had under better control. I'm sure that most of us can relate to gaining a few pounds each Christmas season, but have you ever consciously vowed at the beginning of December to keep that gain to less than a maximum amount? We know we're going to gain the weight, so the question becomes how far out of control we are willing to let it go until we've had enough.

Sometime in my teen years, I vowed to stay under a maximum weight. I knew at the time I wanted to lose a few pounds but I also wanted to ensure that I never went over this maximum because I didn't know how far I might sail by it. If one morning I'm even one pound over this maximum, it triggers a "that's enough" attitude instantly and I do whatever is necessary to take myself back under the maximum. I have also changed my maximum weight over time as my body has changed but I have found that having a goal of what "not to reach" is sometimes as important as a goal to aim for.

My example of weight gain and loss is pretty easy to measure and provides a simple example as it involves dealing only with numbers and watching the scale, but how about that dead-end relationship, friendship, or job? We hope for and work towards a better life for ourselves, doing everything possible to achieve it, but at what point will we know it's sliding negatively and that we've had enough? Try the simple mental exercise of evaluating your life and habits in order to determine a measuring system for your own life.

I truly believe that we should monitor our life as we do our investment portfolios—with quarterly reviews (goal setting and life reviews) and stop losses. Imagine how much more on track our lives would be and how much easier it would be to win at this game we call life.

Specialize but Never Become an Expert

When you're an expert at something, there's only a limited number of ways to do it. When you're new to something, there is an infinite number of ways to do it. Furthermore, the novice is not handicapped by ego—you have nothing to defend and so have no sense of your own self-importance.

When I first took up the sport of golf, I couldn't believe how ridiculously difficult it was to hit a tiny ball with that long and cumbersome club. I remember going to the driving range to learn the basics of the swing and grip. After a lot of practice, I had that all-rewarding connecting hit that made pursuing the sport worthwhile.

Over the years, I have dabbled at taking lessons here and there but since golf takes consistent practice, I've never really improved. My skill is just about the same as it was nearly a decade ago but my ego, with respect to my ability, has certainly increased. Now when I'm at the driving range and someone corrects my swing or suggests a different technique on the course, I greet those comments with resistance and annoyance.

I think that I was actually a better golfer during my first years in the sport because then I was willing to take suggestions from anyone because what's the harm in trying? But now I think I've become an expert and know my own ability and have lost the playful joy a novice experiences.

What's Your Essence?

As Wayne Dyer encourages us to do in his *Manifest Your Destiny*, "Become like the orange." You've likely never thought about it, but no matter what is done to an orange, whether it's squeezed, sliced, or thrown at a wall, the only thing that can come from an orange is orange essence—what it is filled with. What's your essence? Do you think of yourself as a generally calm person but when squeezed and pressed and stressed, you fly off the handle?

I love being an observer at friendly socials or Christmas parties when individuals partake in the alcoholic beverages offered and often have a little too much. You'll likely agree with me that once the guard of the shy wallflower is down, with the blame placed on the cocktails, that person is often the life of the party. Or what about that timid guy who feels ready to take on the world and fight the entire room after two Rum & Cokes? My particular favourite is the live-by-the-book person who never shows any emotion but who, after the third glass of champagne, just *loves* complete strangers.

Going back to my golf example, I have also found the golf course to be a wonderful venue for determining a person's essence. And I'm not alone as more and more corporations are taking key executives out for a game of golf before hiring them or offering opportunities for advancement.

I think everyone should at least try the sport of golf. The game teaches patience and how to get along with others. You will probably have three other people with whom you will be walking the course for four to five hours but, at the end of the day, it's a game all about you. It's kind of like life!

In life, as with golf, there will be many times when no one is watching and it's really easy to cheat. If you find your ball has landed in a bad lie, you can just kick it onto the green or out of the severe rough or you can forget to count the three swings you took in the sand when no one was really looking. The question isn't about the opportunities to cheat and take shortcuts; the question is whether you do. And if you do—in golf or in life—you're just cheating yourself. This particular sport can also reveal a person's attitude when faced with adversity or less-than-ideal conditions. Does the individual remain positive in spite of a poor performance, bad weather, and unruly fellow golfers? Or will three poor holes have the golfer wrapping a club around the nearest tree?

We can blame our poor behaviours and attitudes, whether in golf or in life, on many things but at the end of the day, we can really only control these behaviours and attitudes of ours. We can't control the weather on our wedding day or guarantee that our kids are going to behave this week or that our partner will love us, but we can control our reactions to any situation. So getting back to the example of the orange, what are you filled with? Does it matter how you're squeezed to determine your essence?

There's Always Someone Watching

More people are watching than you think—customers, co-workers, and suppliers. Many times it's not the boss who's noticing your achievements or your slacking or late arrivals, but often someone is watching and it could hurt your future. If all of your co-workers suddenly left and opened up a shop similar to the one where you work now, would you be the first on their list to bring over or would you be dead last? Remember that you might not report to these people, they might not sign your paycheque, but a future employer or someone you might like to have as your own customer one day could be among them. Are you burning bridges without even realizing it?

Take the time and the opportunity to create the policies of your new corporation and watch your success soar, and remember that you have the same 24 hours as the billionaires of the world, so make each moment count and start planning to win now.

> I want to be thoroughly used up when I die,
> for the harder I work the more I live.
> I rejoice in life for its own sake.
> –George Bernard Shaw

Summary

- Hold yourself to a higher standard. Whether you're already a businesswoman or an employee, start thinking of yourself as the president of your personal corporation.
- Know more about your assets than your liabilities and get acquainted with your personal inventory.
- Develop the policies of You, Inc. You won't know when you're breaking one of your own rules if you've never taken the time to create them.
- Remember that you come first and the customer always comes second.

- Your words have awesome power and have the ability to change your thoughts and beliefs in an instant. Choose carefully and be aware in your self-talk and in your communication with others.
- Specialize but don't ever become an expert. Stay open to new possibilities and ideas by remaining a novice of life.

Your Prosperity Action Steps

- Complete Self-Assessment #3
- Complete the "Determining Your Ideal Job" questionnaire.
- List your corporate career goals and put them in writing. Goal conflicts might reveal obvious areas for adjusting your goals.
- As You, Inc., determine what's most important in running your personal corporation. What's your corporate mission statement? What personal policies do you need to examine or develop and refine?
- List an inventory of everything you enjoy and at which you excel. Know more about your assets than your liabilities. Enlist the assistance of your friends, family, and associates to point out your strengths and abilities that you've overlooked.
- What's your ideal or perfect day? List the details and then use the basic NLP skills to more effectively actualize your goals.
- Expand your vocabulary. Define at least ten adjectives to describe your life experiences in positives ways. Learning and reminding ourselves of new words is simple and expands new feelings and therefore experiences in life as a result of our refined word power.
- Make feedback your friend. Start a feedback binder and add to every experience that could use improvement. Be specific and objective. Feedback really is a lifelong friend.

- Be someone new today. Drive to or from work using a different path, shake up your morning routine and try the opposite, or step into the shoes of someone you'd like to be. Remember, flexibility will open your eyes to new opportunities.

Conclusion

I hope you've enjoyed the journey to your prosperity. If I've been successful in guiding you on this journey, you will realize what a special and valuable person you are.

As artist Nathaniel Emmons declared, habit is either the best of servants or the worst of masters. To fully experience *The Woman's Guide to Money*, completing or (at the very minimum) trying the exercises included within this book is paramount; they will help you create new and prosperous habits and beliefs. These in turn will create powerful actions that, when consistently taken, will transform your life in miraculous ways. If you're like the person I used to be and you've skipped over the exercises thinking that it's enough to just experience them mentally, I can assure you that you'll miss the benefits and the entire purpose of this program.

If you need the assistance of a friend or a support group to help motivate you in finishing the exercises, consider starting one today and visit my web site for a complete kit to starting your own book club or support group at www.thewomansguidetomoney.com. You'll not only instill the material deeper within your subconscious by teaching it but you'll also create accountability by completing the exercises with your peers.

I have also included a convenient checklist at the end of the book so you can quickly review the exercises and ensure that you've completed all of them. Use this easy reference guide as an annual tradition and prosperity guide. Use a new journal each year and make a special appointment with yourself to review last year's journal. I'm sure you'll be pleasantly surprised at how very far you've come.

I hope that you will share your successes and challenges with me. Although we have never met, we already share a strong connection. I'm grateful that you've taken the time and allowed me the opportunity to share parts of my life and my philosophy of life with you. It has been my honour and privilege, and I truly wish you success and happiness.

Most of all, my wish for you is that you achieve all that you desire and that you always remember that you are a special and unique person. Also, I want you to realize that you really deserve all that your heart desires and that you are already a successful and valuable human being, whatever your financial status.

Start tapping into the miracles and tools that are available to you now. May God bless you on your journey.

Live prosperously,

Kelley

Your Prosperity Action Steps Checklist

Check each item that you've completed. If you haven't completed an item, indicate your estimated date of completion.

Chapter One: The Inner Game

__ Have I completed Self-Assessment Questionnaire #1?

__ Have I purchased my personal journal for documenting my Prosperity Action Steps?

Chapter Two: Let's Play

__ Have I completed Self-Assessment Questionnaire #2?

__ Have I written down the question "Am I willing to be wealthy," listened carefully, and recorded my thoughts and self-talk?

__ Have I played the $1,000 per day game for at least one week worth of spending?

Chapter 3: Understanding the Laws

__ Have I started my mental cleanse; am I wearing an elastic band?

__ At the end of my day, have I written down three things today and everyday that I am grateful for?

__ In the morning, today and every day, have I written down three things on which I would like to focus my attention?

__ Have I tried a random act of kindness?

__ Have I e-mailed Kelley my ideas for acts of kindness and my success in spreading kindness?

__ Have I e-mailed my friends about the economy game and taught the principles to at least one friend?

Chapter Four: The Bank – Your Saviour?

__ Have I opened my bank accounts and determined how many I would like to have and what I'll name each of them?

__ Have I taught at least one friend the Five Bank Account system?

__ Have I listed at least fifty actions or activities that I will engage in when I'm financially independent?

__ Have I assisted others by e-mailing Kelley my progress with the above list?

__ Have I purchased my piggy bank and started depositing at least $1 per day?

Chapter Five: The Plan

__ Have I defined and documented what success specifically means to me?

__ Have I written my personal mission statement?

__ Have I typed or written out the Daily Success Formula and taped it to my bathroom mirror for at least thirty days?

__ Have I detailed and documented the action steps that I will take for each part of the Daily Success Formula?

__ Have I documented what one thing I will do each week to better use my time?

__ Have I re-read step eight in detail and set my goals on paper?

__ Have I practiced becoming a better movie director at least once this week?

__ Have I booked an appointment with my family and friends in pursuit of becoming a student of life?

Chapter Six: Fear Factor

__ Have I decided what I am willing to change in my environment to support my healthy existence?

__ Have I scheduled time each week for inevitable worries, fears, and time for problem solving?

__ Have I scheduled a recap session each week and listed all of the negative emotions and my new time rules surrounding each?

__ Have I listed what I'm fearful of trying or accomplishing and detailed an action plan with at least ten solutions?

Chapter Seven: You, Inc.

__ Have I completed Self-Assessment Questionnaire #3?

__ Have I completed the "Determining My Ideal Job" questionnaire?

__ Have I listed my corporate career goals and put them in writing? Have I taken the time to review possible goal conflicts?

__ Have I determined my personal policies for You, Inc.? Have I documented those policies?

__ Have I created a detailed list of my personal assets?

__ Have I taken the time to daydream about my perfect day and documented the details of it?

__ Have I used the NLP tools to make my goals more compelling?

__ Have I expanded my vocabulary? Have I defined at least ten adjectives to describe my life experiences in new and positive ways?

__ Have I made feedback my friend? Have I started my feedback binder?

__ Have I stepped into someone else's shoes today, dressed differently, or taken a new path home from work?

I'd love to hear from you! Visit my web site at www.thewomansguidetomoney.com and share your experiences and successes with me today!

Acknowledgements

After many years of lecturing on the subject of "foundational" financial thinking, the success and feedback from those who read *The Prosperity Factor*, I am privileged to have had the opportunity to put my ideas and concepts into written form again.

This book, as with any life project, would have never happened without the encouragement, assistance, and love I received from so many people.

First and foremost, thanks to my incredible mother, Kathleen. If there are angels that walk among us, you're one of them. Thank you for your wisdom, love, and efforts in helping me finish this book and for cheering me along every step of the way. As Abraham Lincoln so eloquently stated: "All that I am, all that I've been, and all that I'll ever be, I owe to my mother."

My heartfelt thanks to the love of my life, Wyatt Cavanaugh. The notion of whom you choose to spend your time with has certainly has benefited me since knowing you. This has been as much a labour of your love as it has mine. My eternal gratitude for introducing me to—and using your brilliance to improve—the ideas and concepts in this book. You never gave up on this project, and I am so grateful for your love and strength in supporting me throughout.

To my amazing family, without whom I could never have had the courage to start this project. When you have a family and support system like I've been blessed with, it makes writing about abundance and prosperity a relatively easy task. My gratitude to my brother David for his life-long intellectual debates, love and support, without which I wouldn't have grown as much as a human and spiritual being. To my brother Randy and his wife, Elaine, and my beautiful nieces, Amelia, Alyshia, Jocelyn, and my little buddy Adam. I hope to have a family as amazing as this one. Thank you all for your love and understanding of the time commitment it takes to write three books in just over one year. To my father, Edward, for teaching me to think, and for a lifelong love of learning.

To my stepfather, Ewald Dreger, who epitomized prosperity and abundance in my life. I miss you and wish you were still here. To two very special women who left footprints of love on my heart: Maggie Halabi and Jaccee Cavanaugh. I miss you both dearly and will always remember your generous spirits and love.

To all of my close and wonderful friends, family, and supporters of this book and *The Prosperity Factor* (in no particular order) who have listened to me talk about this book, supported me emotionally throughout the process, and offered their assistance and ideas freely. I'm so grateful for all of the teachers that I have met on my thirty-year journey on this blue planet. To acknowledge all that have altered my path would take more pages than this total book. I extend my heartfelt thanks to those who have specifically supported this book: Bonnie Lopushinsky, Lisa McMyn, Helene Walker, Jacqueline Young, Catherine Kuehne, Donna Roth, Bill and Melanie Rosser, Brian Rosser, Wesley Schneider, Tracy Scanks, Alex Lakusta, Con and Rose Boland, Amy Sahota, Seanna Collins, Sherry Draper, Carl Sawyer, Gail Greenwood, John Beaudin, Crystal Dallner, Steve and Sharon Budnarchuk, and the amazing staff at Audreys Books. And to my very special four-legged pals, Rusty, Thoreau, Voltaire, Oscar, and Mr. Howls.

To my many clients, students, and, of course, all those who took the time to write me with their ideas, stories, and leanings from *The Prosperity Factor*. I've grown in knowledge as we've learned from each other. Thank you for allowing me to explore my passion with you.

To my many mentors—I owe you thanks, praise, and admiration: Wayne Taylor, Mike Cooney, David Clattenburg, and David Chilton for his words of wisdom.

To my wonderful publisher and the editors at

Insomniac Press, without whom this book would never have been published. I express my extreme gratitude to Mike O'Connor and Dan Varrette. Thank you for believing in this project.

To all of the women who walked before me and made it possible for a woman to have the choice to express herself freely.

In saving the best for last, my heartfelt thanks to my creator, God, for allowing me to be born in a time and country that embraces equality and freedom for women and all who seek it. I am truly blessed!

About the Author

Kelley Keehn, EPC, has been a successful investment professional, retirement planner, and speaker for over a decade. Early in her career, she began to study the underlying principles of the wealthy. Her continuous research was first presented in her impactful Prosperity Factor courses and released in her first book, *The Prosperity Factor for Women*.

Kelley is working on a series of books, can be seen lecturing across Canada and in the U.S., and is a columnist with a number of publications. She is an Elder Planning Counselor (EPC) and is also a faculty member at the Canadian Initiative for Elder Planning Studies (CIEPS). For a complete background on Kelley and where to find her, visit www.thewomansguidetomoney.com.

Kelley resides in Edmonton, Alberta, Canada with Wyatt and their pampered four-legged friends, Thoreau, Voltaire, Oscar, and Mr. Howls.